DIEGO RIVERA
ARTIST OF THE PEOPLE

DIEGO RIVERA
ARTIST OF THE PEOPLE

BY ANNE E. NEIMARK

HarperCollins*Publishers*

DIEGO RIVERA, ARTIST OF THE PEOPLE

Copyright © 1992 by Anne E. Neimark
All rights reserved. No part of this book may be
used or reproduced in any manner whatsoever without
written permission except in the case of brief quotations
embodied in critical articles and reviews.
Printed in the United States of America.
For information address HarperCollins Children's Books,
a division of HarperCollins Publishers,
10 East 53rd Street, New York, NY 10022.
Typography by Elynn Cohen
1   2   3   4   5   6   7   8   9   10
First Edition

Library of Congress Cataloging-in-Publication Data
Neimark, Anne E.
    Diego Rivera, artist of the people / by Anne E. Neimark.
        p.   cm.
    Summary: Follows the life of the twentieth-century Mexican muralist,
from his earliest artistic expressions through his developmental years in
Spain, Paris, and Italy to his political activities when he returned to
Mexico.
    ISBN 0-06-021783-9. — ISBN 0-06-021784-7 (lib. bdg.)
    1. Rivera, Diego, 1886–1957—Juvenile literature.   2. Painters—
Mexico—Biography—Juvenile literature.   [1. Rivera, Diego, 1886–1957.
2. Artists.]   I. Title.
ND259.R5N37   1992   91-25209
759.972—dc20   CIP
[B]   AC

To Kristine and Cathy—
family treasures

ACKNOWLEDGMENTS

◻

My thanks to the Detroit Institute of Arts for allowing me access to Diego's wall murals on a weekend when the mezzanine room was closed—and to Chet Edwards, psychotherapist and expert in the artwork of children, for his valuable and profound insights into Diego's character.

—A.E.N.

LIST OF ILLUSTRATIONS

Self-Portrait, 1930
Diego Rivera's drawing at age three of a train that passed
through Guanajuato, Mexico, *1889*
Woman's head, drawn by Rivera at age twelve, *1898*
The House on the Bridge, 1909
Zapata Landscape—The Guerrilla, 1915
Foundry, 1923
Night of the Rich, 1926
Portrait of Lupe Marín, 1938
Frida and Diego Rivera, 1931
Liberation of the Peon, 1931
South wall of Diego's Detroit industry murals, *1933*
Photograph of Diego Rivera sketching the
Rockefeller Center mural, *1933*
Photograph of screen covering Diego Rivera's mural at
Rockefeller Center, *1933*
Frida's *Self-Portrait, 1940*

color insert, following page 52
La Piñata, 1953
Flower Day, 1925
The Totonac Civilization, 1950
The Bandit Augustín Lorenzo, 1936

AUTHOR'S NOTE

▣

Diego Rivera, born on December 8, 1886, was able to express his deepest concerns for human dignity and possibility through his art. Only by actually viewing his walls can one truly comprehend the amazing vastness of his painted world. Yet I wanted to bring readers a sense of his marvelous murals and paintings as well as of his intriguing life story. Diego's autobiography and writings, and the memories and memoirs of his friends, family members, and even adversaries, all provided helpful material. Some of these sources are listed in the Bibliography and will give readers further knowledge of Diego.

This book is a fictionalized biography. I have invented some of the scenes and dialogues, but they are faithful to Diego as I came to know him. Diego himself fictionalized many events of his life through his tall tales, told against the colorful backgrounds of Spain, France, the U.S.S.R., the United States—and, most of all, Mexico.

SELF-PORTRAIT *Diego Rivera.* 1930. Collection, The Museum of Modern Art, New York.   Gift of Abby Aldrich Rockefeller.

DIEGO RIVERA
ARTIST OF THE PEOPLE

CHAPTER ONE

◫

THE SUN WAS STILL SLEEPING IN Guanajuato, Mexico. A purple haze hung over cobblestone streets, drifted drowsily across flat-roofed houses, lifted a tendril or two toward the hills. Inside Señor Rivera's house on Pocitos Street, three-year-old Diego crept from his bed. Grabbing a red crayon, he tiptoed down a hall toward the front door.

The blank wall flanked the doorway, white and inviting. In the shadows, Diego waited for the sun. Where was its golden heat? When would it make the morning? Turning the crayon in his hand, he touched it to the wall. He would bring the sun *now*, keep it inside always. Papa, Mama, and Aunt Vicenta would not scream; only his aunt Cesaría might scream.

With the crayon, he began the circle. Red, thick—a fiery blaze on white wall. Curves of color, darkest at the center.

Then a pause while Diego's wide-set, protruding eyes—his aunt Cesaría called him *carasapo* (frog face)—carefully scanned his creation. There must be heat beyond the circle, a light red from rubbing the side of the crayon on the wall. Then a mountaintop nearby, dotted with prickly cactuses; then a . . .

"*DIEGO!*" came Aunt Cesaría's shout. "*Dios mío*, what are you doing? María, wake up! Look at your child. He's ruining the wall!"

Quickly, they were all upon him. Papa, in his black beard and nightshirt; Mama, so pale and short beside him; Aunt Vicenta and Aunt Cesaría in bedtime gowns. "Diego, Diego," moaned his mother. "You must not do that."

"You had three stillbirths, María," said Aunt Cesaría. "Then twin boys, one soon dead. Why God left you with Diego, not his little twin, Carlos—who is to know?"

"Diego's not a bad boy," said his father, Señor Diego Rivera. "He has his imaginings. When I taught school, when I became city councilor, I saw some bad boys. Diego is just—Diego."

Aunt Cesaría had filled a bucket with soapy water and was trying furiously to scrub Diego's sun off the wall. Aunt Vicenta was gathering pieces of drawing paper so that Diego could have "proper materials." Diego's mother knelt before a statue of the Virgin Mary on the parlor mantel, quietly praying.

"Mama!" Diego called. "Do not pray to the wooden statue.

4

She's silly. She has no holes in her ears. She cannot hear you. I only drew on the wall because my friends told me to do it!"

"*Dios mío!*" screamed Aunt Cesaría. "He's a monster. He pokes fun at the Virgin Mary and sometimes—forgive me—at God. And he *lies*. He blames imaginary friends for the drawings—pencil and crayon marks on everything, on the tablecloths, on the household bills, on my lace handkerchief!"

"Enough!" said Señor Rivera, hoisting Diego onto a chair. "I have decided. In a few days, the new decade begins—the 1890's. In honor of possibilities, I give the guest room to Diego. All the furniture will go. I will nail blackboards over the walls. Diego can draw and draw—and I'll have complaints from no one."

"A whole room for this tiny, frog-faced monster?" shrieked Aunt Cesaría, shaking her head until a scatter of hairpins tumbled to the floor. "But he lies! He makes lies! What, pray tell, is ever to become of him?"

He liked machines best of all. Of course, he was five years old now, pudgier, his eyes even larger. He drew locomotives with cabooses carrying silver ore from Guanajuato's mines; he lay on his back in his blackboard room imagining the interiors of steamboat engines. Then he drew steamboats on his blackboards or a mining machine, cracked open and rusting, that he'd seen in the hills with Aunt Vicenta.

He liked to know the insides of *everything*. On Saturdays, his father disappeared with Don Trinidad, the foreman of the

Diego's drawing at age three of a train that passed through Guanajuato, Mexico. 1889. Museo Anahuacalli, Mexico, D.F.

only silver mine still owned by the family, to study ore samples. What was inside the ore? Why was his father so worried about the mine—or about keeping his job as councilor? "I lobby for more village schools," his father said. "My welcome grows among my poor Indian peasant friends—but not among government officials." *Why?* Diego wondered. Why didn't the government like the peasants? Why didn't it like his father?

A year before, in his parents' bedroom, Diego had found a Spanish textbook written by his father. "What does it say, Papa?" he'd asked. "Teach me to read." And in Aunt Vicenta's room, he'd discovered a locked treasure chest. Persuading his aunt to open it, he'd rummaged hungrily among the Mexican artifacts: burnished silver and tortoiseshell jewelry, lacquered belt buckles, glazed pottery and colorful embroideries, *retablos*, small religious paintings, that offered thanks for salvation from various misfortunes. What wondrous objects to be copied in chalk onto his blackboards! So much color and shine!

One entire morning and afternoon, he did not draw. On a Sunday, two months after his birthday—the eighth of December—when his mother had confided that the "gift" of a baby sister or brother would be coming, his Aunt Vicenta had taken him to the railway station. "Today, your little brother arrives by train in a box," Aunt Vicenta told him. "You must stay here to receive him, Diego. I will help your mother clean house."

All day Diego waited for the train. The station platform was bare; mines were yielding less silver, so few freight cars of ore still passed through Marfil Station, and miners no longer gathered along the platform with their gourds of *pulque* wine. Diego didn't want to wait for a baby brother. What if the baby grew up to steal his crayons or chalk? Sitting down on a bench at the station house, he swung his legs back and forth. Usually he loved to be near the trains. Their clang and clatter would sing through his dreams. But now he was cold and sleepy. Was he supposed to carry the baby home in its box without dropping it *once*?

At dusk, the passenger train finally appeared, only to blast its whistle, not grinding to a stop. Stunned, Diego rose from the bench. He had waited for nothing. Slowly, he started walking home toward Pocitos Street, the hills seeming to close in on Guanajuato like petals. Crumbling a piece of chalk from his pocket into a long yellow trail on the cobblestones, he was silent as he entered the foyer of his house, silent when Aunt Vicenta saw him.

"Diego!" she said. "You'll never guess what happened! The baby was delivered *here* in its box, not by train but by wagon. And it's a sister, named María after your mother!"

In his parents' bedroom, Diego found his mother beneath the thick patchwork quilt, her face damp in the light from a bedside candle. "Where is the baby's box, Mama?" Diego demanded. "Where have you put it?"

María del Pilar Barrientos de Rivera gestured weakly toward a blanket-covered lump beside her on her husband's pillow. "Oh," she said, "come look at your sister, Diego. I don't know where the box is. It doesn't matter."

But Diego would not be distracted. "The box, Mama!" he insisted. "First I must see the box."

Running, then bending, yanking, climbing, reaching into drawers, crawling into closets, he searched the house. He would not be stopped, but he unearthed no new boxes, nothing to hold a baby. At last, his own face as damp as his mother's, he confronted her again. "You also tell lies, Mama," he said. "Aunt Vicenta, too. The baby wasn't on the train. You sent me away so I couldn't see it arrive."

"Don't be sad, Diego," coaxed his mother. "Rejoice with us that you have a sister."

"Did she come from inside you, Mama?" he asked. "Is that why you were so fat?"

A hand on his shoulder spun him sideways. "No more questions, Diego," said Aunt Cesaría. "Even frogs must stop croaking. Let your mother rest. Go draw your pictures."

Too restless to fill his blackboards, Diego escaped into the kitchen. Bananas and mangoes, ripe in their clay bowl, did not tempt him—nor did the floured tortillas on the wooden table. But a dark flash of gray on the floor captivated him at once: a field mouse, scurrying across the stones, tail tapered like a shoelace. Diego dropped to his knees, crawling after the mouse until it darted into a corner. Seizing its tail, he swung the small, furry creature into the air, surprised by the pink swell of belly.

The mouse was fat as Diego's mother had been fat. What was in its stomach? Food—or, perhaps, baby mice? How would they be born? Could he draw a birth? Would the mouse's belly unbutton like a sweater?

Holding tightly to the long tail, Diego stood up. In the sink was a small knife, its blade serrated with tiny notches. Once, with his father, he'd visited a mud-baked peasant hut on the hilly rim of Guanajuato, but he was kept outside. A baby was being born; he'd heard cries and grunting. A man wearing a dirty sombrero carried a knife into the hut, muttering about "cutting the cord." Diego hadn't understood. How was the knife used in the baby's birth? On the ride home, his father spoke only of poverty and disease among the peasants—of something called "injustice."

Turning the squirming mouse on its back on the sink board, Diego pricked the pink, rounded belly with the tip of the knife. *Insides*, he thought, had more secrets than *outsides*. If he opened up the mouse, would he know reasons and answers—would he know where babies hid?

As one dot of blood stained his finger, he heard the familiar shouts. *"Dios mío! Dios mío!"* screamed Aunt Cesaría. "Now what has he done?" Startled, Diego let the mouse catapult to the floor. It squealed, rolled over onto its feet, and careened behind the iron stove for safety. Then Diego's father was looming large in the doorway, watching his son drop the knife in the sink. "A mouse is not a machine," said his father. "You mustn't hurt it just to see inside or because you're angry. Come, we will open my anatomy books instead. You will find drawings. You will understand about mice and about babies."

Diego walked past the bowl of ripe bananas and mangoes, past the tortillas on the kitchen table, past the stove that had become a sudden mouse sanctuary. But he couldn't avoid the look of horror on his Aunt Cesaría's face. "Devil," she whispered. "Monster! You bring shame to this house, shame to the birth of your sister."

He did not answer. Contrite, he lowered his huge eyes, the lids stretching to cover them. He hadn't meant to ruin his sister's birth, was sorry to have hurt the mouse. He had learned to put his drawings on surfaces that didn't cause any screams; he had tried to obey. But if he couldn't *know*, he wanted to tell his aunt, how could he draw? And if he couldn't *draw*—how could he be Diego?

CHAPTER TWO

◻

THE FAMILY WAS MOVING TO
Mexico City—the "City of Palaces" of Mexico's
president-dictator, Porfirio Díaz. Foreign dignitaries
were escorted through Díaz's French-style palaces and cathedrals, Italian-style opera house and post office. Tours never
included a glimpse of the country's destitute Indian peasants,
descendents of once-proud civilizations.

None of the Riveras was happy to move. The family mine
was barren, however, and Señor Rivera had angered Guanajuato's wealthy landowners and merchants, even leaders in
Mexico's Catholic church, by writing a weekly newsletter, *El
Democrata*. The paper demanded land rights, education, and
sanitation for the poor. Unfortunately, peasants who might
have embraced *El Democrata* didn't know how to read it. And

Guanajuato's "decent folk," as the wealthy were called, wanted nothing to do with Señor Rivera's "crazy Liberal notions."

In Mexico City, Diego missed what he had loved in Guanajuato: the purple hills, the winding streets, the trains, the clutter of mining machines. In Mexico City, the Rivera house was too small for a "blackboard room" for Diego. He was miserable and sick, first with scarlet fever, then typhoid and diphtheria. Covered with rashes or delirious from fevers, he lay in bed by a wall—a blank, whitewashed wall with no crayoned sun on it. "I'm not to draw," he told his aunt Vicenta. "My friends came in the night on mules. They ordered me to be sick."

"Ah, Diego," cautioned Aunt Vicenta. "Seven years old— too old for such lies. These friends are just noise in your head. Let me read to you from your papa's books."

Being read to by his aunt distracted Diego from the rashes and fevers. She always let him select books from his father's shelves, never pushed "baby tales" on him. He would choose texts on history, medicine, travel, adventure, science, and social reform. Staring over his aunt's elbow at a history book, he marveled at drawings of soldiers with their muskets and cannons. War fascinated him: the battle plans, the swift attacks. He imagined the pummeling sounds of both victory and defeat.

When the doctor said he was well enough to eat with his little sister, Diego began to draw again. He sketched hundreds of soldiers on cardboard his father gave him—uniformed figures carrying guns, riding fiercely on horses, marching in military formation. He cut out soliders until he had five hundred of them across the floor, enough to tempt several neighbor boys, who asked if they could play war.

On paper, he charted military battles, drawing elaborate maps and devising escapes. Military careers were prized in Mexico. His father was so impressed with Diego's charting that he showed it to an old friend, General Pedro Hinojoso, Minister of War. Amazed, the general promised to shepherd Diego's future in the army. But when, at age ten, Diego was sent to military preparatory school in Mexico City, he destroyed his cardboard soldiers within a week. "What hateful rules!" he told his father. "The school makes us drill for hours. I can't stop to see the sky. Don't send me back, Papa. I won't go back!"

A military life was not to be. Diego's mother, praying beneath her mantel statue of the Virgin Mary, saw a chance for her son's salvation and insisted he enter Catholic school. Diego tried to conform; report cards praised his intelligence, and at the Liceo Católico Hispano-Mexicano, he often won first place in examinations. Two priests even vied for the privilege of instructing him in Catholic doctrine. Yet, exposed to the dogma of the catechism, he badgered Padre Enrique with questions, causing the priest to rethink having been "awarded" this bright but impudent child.

One day, upon hearing of the virgin birth, Diego defiantly

shook his head. "A lie, Padre!" he said. "I *know* how babies come. If the Virgin Mary expelled baby Jesus from her body, why was she still thought a virgin?"

Shocked by such an outrageous question, Padre Enrique grasped Diego firmly by the hand and, with the headmaster's permission, took him to the Rivera house. "Your son," the priest told Diego's mother, "has a lightning-swift mind. Nevertheless, our school faculty believes he should receive religious training at home. We must not disturb the other students."

Diego's mother, nodding sadly, considered her pudgy, bulbous-eyed child. She loved him, but sometimes she was a bit afraid of him. He would do things that should not be done, say things that should not be said—even if her husband assured her that "Diego was just . . . *Diego*." Crossing herself, María Rivera vowed that, on this very night—after everyone was asleep—she would kneel in wrinkled sackcloth and ashes before the mantel and offer the Virgin Mary a special prayer, a novena, in her ten-year-old Diego's name.

His curiosity had become as focused as pencil tip on paper. All the wondering, looking, and questioning had served his urge to draw. Guanajuato's mining machines had shown him the interlocking of gears; faces in Mexico City's markets had taught him about bone structure and skin; soldiers pictured in battle in his father's books had revealed rippling muscles under stress. All this he had used, like fuel for his own machine: to create shapes on flat surfaces, to make forms true to their inner structure.

"I want," he told his family before his eleventh birthday, breath caught in his throat, "to go to art school." He flushed at his aunt Cesaría's snort, her "We don't need to waste money on your little scribbles," but he did not retreat. He promised to stay faithfully in regular school if he could attend art school at night. He promised to earn high marks, not to annoy his teachers, not to "invent stories." Anxiously, he watched his aunt Vicenta smile indulgently, his mother make another sign of the cross, his father hesitate, start to speak, hesitate—and then . . . give in.

At the San Carlos Academy of Fine Arts, Diego was the youngest student. In regular school, he strained for the hours to rush by toward the moment when he could race down Santa Inés to the art school's entrance and be met by a smell of oil paint and the sight of canvases and palettes. He listened raptly to the weighty lectures on composition, proportion, line, and color. In the workrooms, he walked among copies of classical European paintings—revered by President Díaz, as were all art and architecture from Europe. Sketching, drawing, and painting; erasing, blotting out, and with instruction from his professors, starting again, Diego spent two happy school terms at San Carlos before he began resenting the stiff discipline.

In drawing he won second prize, a small box of oil paints he carried with him to paint outdoors. He studied Aztec sculpture, awed by its massive gargoyles and serpents. One of his professors, an old Mexican artist named Santiago Rebull, took an interest in Diego despite jealous taunts of his classmates. Rebull talked of "movement" in painting, of putting onto canvas what is fluid in life, of showing tension in muscle even in a standing figure or in the leaning of grass against the pressure of wind. "A painting," Rebull said to Diego, "should contain perpetual movement. You are young, my boy—but if you ever amount to anything, it will be because you've captured movement."

In 1899, Diego turned thirteen; he had finished elementary school and was awarded a San Carlos scholarship of thirty pesos per month. The money would pay his tuition as a full-time day student. He was always drawing and painting; a sketch he made at age twelve of a woman's head showed a maturity of style far beyond his years. Not all of his training, however, came from professors at San Carlos or from the tedious exercises of copying shapes from plaster casts. In the carriage entrance near the Church of Santa Inés was the tiny shop of José Posada, an engraver who printed and illustrated popular folk songs and prayers treasured by Mexico's poor. Inside Posada's shop, Diego first heard of art "for the people."

Fastening wooden blocks onto a rickety press to print *calaveras* (illustrated song sheets), Posada welcomed Diego's visits. "Art can be learned in the streets," Posada explained, "not just in fancy studios and salons. Peasants crowd the markets for my *calaveras*. If a peasant can't read, he'll find someone who can. He'll look at the engraved drawings. Your eyes, Diego, are big enough to see Truth: Art can lift up the

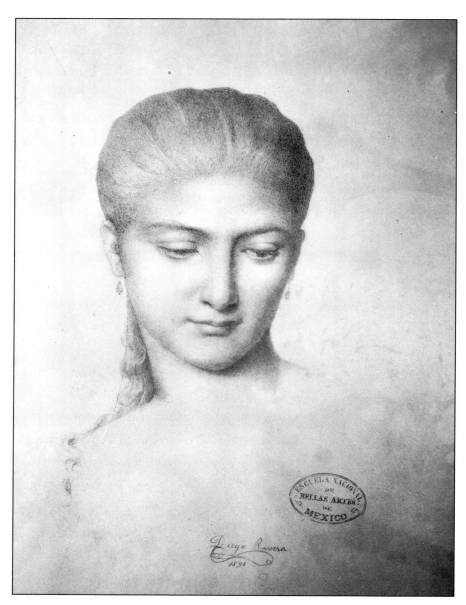

A woman's head drawn by Diego at twelve years of age. 1898. Escuela Nacional de Artes Plásticas, UNAM. Mexico City, Mexico.

downtrodden, teach them to change their fate."

When he was fifteen, Diego was seized by the same concern for social reform as his father and José Posada. Wandering the marketplaces, he studied the simple folk art—baskets and pottery, clay figures and toys, handwoven shawls, sandals and sashes. At San Carlos, noted for its fine art, such objects were considered vulgar, the handwork of peasants. Diego, however, admired these colorful creations. From childhood, he had questioned established rules and rigidities; now he would do more.

A new director at San Carlos, Antonio Fabres, had been abruptly installed by an aging President Díaz. Students secretly criticized a president and cabinet who were in their seventies and eighties. They objected more openly when Director Fabres kept relying on European art traditions of indoor rather than outdoor painting, of religious subject matter over more commonplace themes. They gossiped in the corridors about a corrupt priest who hadn't been dismissed. Diego, with José Posada's advice buzzing in his head, suddenly became the ringleader of a revolt.

On a July morning in 1902, Diego arrived at San Carlos with posters he'd painted, some demanding Director Fabres's resignation, others calling for the discharge of the scandalous priest. Goading a dozen classmates to follow him into the street, Diego passed the posters among them. "Let's march!" he urged. "Protest! Let's fight for our causes!"

Whistling and yelling in agreement, the students held

Diego's posters aloft and fell into line behind him. The "Rivera Demonstration," as it would be dubbed, wove down busy Santa Inés, catching the attention of passersby and drawing a crowd. Waving to José Posada, who watched, grinning, from his shop, Diego saw several faculty members from San Carlos scrambling along the curb. "Stop!" they shouted at him. "Insufferable, Rivera! You'll be punished!"

A feeling of pride, however—not of shame or fear—thrust Diego onward. He knew that if his aunt Cesaría had been in the crowd, she'd be wailing *"Monster!"*—but he had his own notions of right and wrong. Even after the demonstration ended and posters were left as wrinkled reminders on the steps of San Carlos, even after a scowling Director Fabres arrived at the Rivera house, Diego was not afraid.

"Your son," said the Director to Diego's father, as had a red-faced Padre Enrique to his mother, "is a talented artist. But he has seriously disrupted our faculty and students. Since he's harmed the reputation of San Carlos, I cannot tolerate his presence. I bring official notice that he is expelled."

A familiar scene materialized in the parlor. Aunt Vicenta sighed, forlornly shaking her head; Aunt Cesaría snorted, hairpins tumbling with one loud *"Dios mío"*; María Rivera hastily crossed herself, turning helplessly with her daughter toward the mantel; and Diego's father, brow furrowing, seemed to wrestle with both rebuke and understanding. In the shadows, Diego stood erect. He was seeing the five people in front of him as if they were sketched on canvas, bending and shifting in a movement that his teacher, Rebull, would have applauded. For a moment, he forgot the reason for everyone's presence in the parlor; he saw only the composition of figures, the geometric planes of line and space, the light, darkness, and shading of tone and color.

Perhaps it was Diego's insistent turning of life into art, of finding, as he would later say, that "forms and colors exist in absolute purity," that eventually would bring this rebellious fifteen-year-old who was expelled from San Carlos an appointment, nearly three decades later, as its director.

CHAPTER THREE

◻

WITH HIS CANVAS PROPPED ON
rocks near Jalapa, capital city of the Mexican
state of Veracruz, Diego squeezed oil paint
onto his palette. Orizaba mountain jutted its volcanic peak
above him into the sky. Although the reddish-brown paint
might recapture Orizaba's earth tones, Diego wasn't certain.
On his sketchpad, in watercolor, his rendering of the mountain satisfied him—but on canvas the paint seemed muddy,
greens darkening like soggy leaves, blues dulled to dirty
grays.

Since his expulsion from San Carlos—and against his parents' wishes—Diego had hitchhiked across Mexico with bags
of art supplies, climbing down canyons and burro trails to
sketch tropical flowers, painting coral reefs at the Peninsula

of Yucatán, where Mayan civilization once flourished, drawing buzzards and monkeys that congregated wherever Indian villagers built their reed huts. His eyes, restless under their thick lids, took him wandering, turning sights into painted stories of volcanoes, jungles, and deserts; of Xochipilli, ancient Aztec god of flowers, of Centeotl, ancient goddess of corn.

He devoured sketchpads and small canvases; his art pencils grew stubby, his paint tubes lay crimped and empty. He wrote home to his parents that he had not drowned or been killed. He did not tell them he worried about his own health. His sight sometimes was cloudy. Would he go blind? But on that day near Jalapa, he decided it was his painting of Orizaba that was clouded. Painted mountain fuzzed into painted sky; fir trees were smudged.

Diego flung his brush into the dirt. He needed more answers. Perhaps he should sail to Europe, where art-minded sons of Mexico's wealthy families went to study. At San Carlos, he had railed against mimicking European art, yet Mexico's beauty and rhythms outpaced him. José Posada had said that art should be learned on the streets, that fashionable salons of Madrid or Paris could be suffocating—but Diego was not convinced.

Behind him, he heard voices and a thrashing sound in the bushes. A group of ragged peasants stumbled toward him, their hands grasping a burlap sling that supported a young boy. Diego peered down at the child's left leg; it wobbled, uncovered, on the sling as if it were disconnected from the hip. Starting at the knee, a wide, pus-filled gash plunged to the ankle. "What happened?" Diego asked the peasant nearest him.

"My son, Carlos, cut his leg," the man answered. "He's very sick. We work all day in the textile mills. Our foreman gives us no time off to care for Carlos."

Diego had seen the dried-mud shacks at the borders of the estates outside Jalapa. Along with the mills, the estates were owned by rich men who treated their workers like slaves. Meager wages were paid not in money but in tokens redeemable only at the company store. "Where are you taking the boy?" Diego asked.

"Nothing in the store cures him," the man said. "We left our shacks without permission. We're bringing Carlos to a cave witch, a healer, on Orizaba's north slope. She removes live toads from foreheads of the bewitched. She casts out the evil eye."

Staring at the ravaged leg with its oozing wound attracting a swarm of flies, Diego dug into his pocket for coins he'd earned sketching portraits in Jalapa's square. "Here," he said, offering the money. "Carlos should see a real doctor."

Carlos's father and the other peasants gently laid the sling on the mossy ground. After a few protests, they gratefully accepted the coins. Carlos, grimacing, rolled slightly to one side so that he could look up at Diego. "How old are you?" he asked softly.

"Sixteen," Diego said. "How old are *you*?"

"Eleven," Carlos answered. Lifting himself with effort onto his elbows, he pointed at the canvas leaning against a rock. "Did you paint the mountain? All by yourself?"

"Yes," Diego said, wishing deeply that the colors were clearer, the fir trees at Orizaba's peak more distinct. Suddenly, he picked up the narrow canvas and balanced it on the burlap beside the boy's healthy leg. "Would you like this?" he said. "I'll give it to you."

Carlos's eyes widened in amazement. Peasant families weren't accustomed to owning anything. "For *me*?" he whispered in disbelief. "To keep?"

"For you," Diego said.

The boy nodded fiercely, glancing at his father for approval and again at Diego. "Thank you," he mumbled. "I don't know anyone who paints. Perhaps your gift will help me feel better." Carlos's father asked Diego to sign the canvas. Then, thanking him for his kindness, the men picked up the sling and went onward. Diego watched the bobbing rim of his canvas; he saw Carlos's trembling fingers reach to touch it. Coins and a canvas, Diego thought, weren't enough. He must learn truly to help the needy. He must paint more than mountains. His work should bring a message—something he might uncover in Europe if he were lucky enough to earn passage.

Catching a last glimpse of Carlos, the boy's left leg twitching against the motion of the burlap, the painted canvas held as if it were magic, Diego bent down toward the dirt and picked up his discarded brush.

□   □   □

25

In the autumn of 1906, Diego returned to Orizaba mountain. His father was now an inspector for Mexico's National Department of Public Health and, during an outbreak of yellow fever in the lowlands, often traveled to Veracruz. Twice, Diego halted his solitary wanderings to go along. Each day, he painted Orizaba. Standing back from his efforts to see if he'd found the way to paint the massive slopes, he remained as restless of heart as he was of eye.

He talked to his father about Europe. Unable to pay passage abroad, Señor Rivera took five of his son's paintings to the governor of Guanajuato, petitioning for an art stipend. But though the Riveras had lived in Guanajuato, the governor refused the request. He had no interest in art. Besides, he grumbled, young Mexicans who fled to Europe developed haughty airs and were lazy.

Back in Veracruz, Señor Rivera told Diego to wait for him in Jalapa. "I have to monitor sanitation at the hospitals," he said. "But I'll talk to Governor Dehesa of Veracruz. He's a Liberal who loves artists and teachers. He's sent other young men abroad."

Setting up his easel on Jalapa's streets, Diego painted women with fruit baskets on their heads and tables of toy skeletons readied for the festive Day of the Dead holiday. As he mixed his paints, however, he heard rumors. Mill workers, barely surviving, had suffered another wage cut. Usually resigned to their fate, they had apparently been pushed too far this time by greedy estate owners.

On a Wednesday, workers abandoned the mills, swarming over the lowlands, drinking *pulque* wine and shaking their fists. By Friday, when hundreds converged on Jalapa, a local group of Spanish and Cuban revolutionaries organized a formal strike. Diego folded up his easel. He saw the grime of the mills on peasant faces and the scars of whippings on sun-scorched backs. He remembered the demonstration he'd led at San Carlos, how easily he'd yelled, "Let's protest!" to class-mates. What would he do now? Take up the peasant cause?

By evening of the fifth day, Jalapa was overrun by peasants. Like a kettle boiling over, workers kept pouring from the fields. Disease-ridden and poor, they had never before re-belled during the regime of Porfirio Díaz. The strike gave them courage. Wives and children joined in, having hiked for miles on bare feet or in torn sandals. Diego gave bites of melon to three little boys who ran, half naked, at his heels. He stroked a louse-infested infant who peeked at him from a bag.

President Díaz was enraged over the strike. Demanding obedience from those he governed, he dispatched troops into Jalapa, formations that galloped in on horseback, brandishing rifles and sabres. At the sight of armed soldiers, Diego plunged into the square. Peasant women were crying, shelter-ing babies in their skirts; workers threw stones or garbage at soldiers, while bursts of gunfire filled the teeming square. Diego heard screams just as he saw blood spurting as if from fountains; bodies dropped, writhing, onto the cobblestones.

Soldiers re-aimed their rifles, shooting at children. Diego kneeled beside a woman who stared up at him and died. Heart pounding, he saw the dark hooves of horses, as everything was turning red, the street a palette of blood.

In the next moments, when an old, crippled peasant was pierced by a sabre, Diego picked up a rock and threw it at a sneering soldier. The sabre slashed the air, grazing the back of Diego's head. Reeling, he was hauled away by other soldiers and tossed into a truck, four peasants heaped beside him. Engine grinding, the truck rattled off, disgorging its contents at Jalapa's jail. Diego was shoved down a corridor and into a cell. Peasants awaited him amid odors of sweat, wine, and vomit. He ripped off part of his shirt and bandaged his head.

By morning, when Señor Rivera arrived at the jail to find his missing son, Diego was eating stale bread in his cell. "Are you badly hurt?" Señor Rivera asked, peering at the makeshift bandage. "Why have you been arrested?"

"I listened to what you taught me, Papa," Diego said. "I've been defending social justice."

His father nodded. "Governor Dehesa will see to your release. The city is in an uproar; a mass grave is being dug for murdered peasants. But in spite of the tragedy, I have amazing news. The governor, Diego, is awarding you a yearly stipend. You'll go to Europe!"

Diego leaned forward. "To Europe?" he repeated. Dizzily, he clutched the jail bars. He would study in Europe? This was not just a story? Leaving Mexico behind would mean leaving his family and the land of his birth. But the answers he was seeking beckoned him from across the seas. "*Thank you*, Papa," he said quickly. "I'll send home paintings to you and to Governor Dehesa. I'll paint enough pictures, I promise, to cover every wall of the governor's house!"

CHAPTER FOUR

□

EUROPE WAS A KALEIDOSCOPE OF
forms and shapes. Diego studied in Madrid under the
honored painter Eduardo Chicharro, entranced by the
work of Spanish artists Pablo Picasso, Juan Gris, El Greco,
Ignacio Zuloaga. He drove himself so furiously, filled canvases so rapidly, that Chicharro's first report on him—sent to
Governor Dehesa—said he had "made much progress which I
do not hesitate to qualify as astounding."

Occasionally, when he did not paint, he hiked the country-
sides of Madrid and Toledo, or made side trips to Portugal,
sketching the sights on postcards sent home. He barely slept,
spending nights in Spanish cafés listening to talk of another
strike, this time by workers in Barcelona. Though he marked
his twenty-first birthday in Spain, he was too exhausted to

celebrate. "Come, Rivera! Drink up!" urged Mexican and Spanish painter friends at a café.

"My head hurts," he said. "And tomorrow I must awaken by five to finish my canvas before Chicharro sees it."

"You have the aches of an old man," snarled one of the painters. "You drink mineral water instead of champagne. How do you stay fat?"

It was true he'd gained weight. He was over six feet tall and grew heavier with the days. His head throbbed and his eyes still clouded. A doctor had diagnosed glandular trouble, recommending mineral water, no meats, plates heaped with lemons. He'd taken to wearing a cowboy hat as a shield against the sun. In spite of Chicharro's praise, his painting could discourage him, as it had when he'd painted Orizaba, and he'd prowl Madrid bookstores, his cowboy hat dipping and rising along the shelves. With his stipend, he bought cheap editions of Darwin, Huxley, Voltaire, Zola, Schopenhauer, and Marx, reading in fits and starts. His hunger for food and for books hid his greater hunger for a style of his own, copied from no one.

Diego's Madrid studio was cluttered with canvases, dozens completed, others discarded in mid effort or just begun. Each dawn, he'd climb tensely among them, palette held high, correcting a false line, a wrong curve. The morning light, startling across his paintings, gave hope of some redeeming achievement—but by nightfall, he might sour again on his creations. He hiked to Toledo to capture on canvas the same river with a bridge that El Greco had painted—but its essence eluded him.

In 1908, Diego took a freighter to London, carrying a sketchpad for his impressions of the industrial city. In London's factory district, he found dingy brick buildings crammed with hordes of impoverished workers. He roamed the streets and trash-filled alleys, renting a room from an old woman with tea-stained teeth. She stared at his cowboy hat, bulging eyes, and oversized, rumpled clothes. "Big one, ain't ya?" she said. "Fill up m' whole doorway. Never seen the likes o' ya."

"Once I . . . Mexican *bandito*," Diego answered in broken English. "Now I seek right life."

"Pay a week's rent," cackled the woman, patting her apron pocket, "and righteousness is yours."

Leaving his knapsack in the room, Diego set out with his sketchpad. Smoke blackened the air as it pulsed from the chimneys. Shops sagged wearily against each other; horses, flicking their tails, were harnessed to lampposts. He wandered down to the docks, watching workers hoist crates onto their shoulders. By nightfall, he'd made fourteen sketches: pale, skinny boys in torn knickers, drunks with swollen noses, pregnant women sweeping grime from tenement steps. He crossed over London Bridge to the Embankment of the Thames, where the homeless were said to sleep. Begging hands stretched out to him. "A few farthings, Mister? Buy us a meal?"

Digging into his pocket, Diego could see himself at age six

when his aunt Vicenta had pleaded with him to leave a coin at church. Stubbornly, he'd refused. "Why does God need money?" he'd confronted his aunt. "You said he makes miracles!" Now Diego felt that to give to the poor *was* miraculous. Pressing coins into roughened palms, he settled down on the Embankment. He told none of the beggars that he was a Mexican painter. If they'd said he, too, must be homeless, he would have agreed. Until he knew more of what he most wanted to paint—and how to paint it—he would not have a real home.

Near dawn, Diego walked back to his rented room. In the hallway of the shingled boardinghouse, he was surprised to find the landlady awake and dragging sacks across the floor. "So early?" he said to her.

"Takin' out the eatin' trash and regular trash," she answered.

"Eatin' trash?" he said.

She opened a small cloth sack, her sparse, white hair clumping over her collar. "See—I separate what ain't poison. Poor people rummage for it in the alley. Strips of fat . . . spoiled apples . . . molded cheese. It's charity."

Diego lifted the sacks into the alley, placing the small one at the top of a splintered trash box. A mush of rancid apples leaked through the cloth onto his fingers. With his cowboy hat tilted over his head, he thought of the paintings of fruit in artists' studios. Apples were perfect, crisply red, full of shine. Licking his fingers, he could taste the sourness of this discarded fruit. José Posada had always scorned the posed "falseness" of studio art. "Paint from your heart for the little people," he'd said. Diego wondered what his own art should say to the homeless who slept by the river Thames.

Paris. He had come by hitchhiking and by railway car to this mecca of artists and writers. While Spain preached traditional techniques in creating art, such as emphasizing dark paint colors and formal studio portraits, Paris whirled with experimentation. French art movements quickly flourished or died. Impressionists—Édouard Manet, Claude Monet, Pierre Renoir, Edgar Degas—often painted outdoors, enamored of nature and the play of light on their subjects. Fauvists—Paul Gauguin, Henri Matisse, André Derain, Georges Rouault—used brilliant colors and bold outlines to depict their subjects. Pointillists like Georges Seurat painted hundreds or even thousands of tiny, tightly placed dots that, when viewed from several feet away, merged smoothly together.

At the Paris railway station, Diego had read his directions for locating the Hotel Suez, popular with artists. He rented a small room there overlooking the Boulevard St. Michel. His money was running low, but he could paint in the city's free art academies, where professors offered instruction. Artists also set up easels along the river Seine and in the area of Montparnasse. Diego would walk to the grand cathedrals of Nôtre Dame and Sacré Coeur; he would view the Arc de Triomphe, Emperor Napoleon's monument to his troops. At night, he'd frequent Paris cafés with starving poets, painters, actors, jugglers, and musicians, with political exiles and self-appointed philosophers who would inspire him to paint like what he called a "*tonto loco* (crazy fool)."

On his second day in Paris, Diego ventured down the Boulevard St. Michel with his page of directions. He found the Galerie Vollard, which displayed the new art trends and techniques. In the window was a painting by the great French artist Paul Cézanne, who'd recently died. Diego was awed. The rendering of an old man with a pipe was as fine as any he'd seen. He didn't budge from the window, pressing his whole face on the glass, his eyes seeming to swell under their lids. All morning, even as rain fell, he stood transfixed before the painting, noting every detail of its unusually sharp angles. Inside the gallery, Monsieur Vollard was perplexed by the young man who stared. Was he a burglar plotting a theft? Someone just released from an asylum?

At noon, shaking his head, Monsieur Vollard left for lunch, returning in an hour to discover Diego still at the window. Exasperated but intrigued, the gallery owner disappeared into a back room just long enough to bring out another painting—also a Cézanne—which he exchanged for the first one. Diego was breathing in gasps as if he couldn't get enough air. The excitement of seeing such genius on a damp street in Paris was overwhelming. He was worlds away from Mexico, but he wished his old teachers, Rebull and Posada, were with him.

Throughout the afternoon, Monsieur Vollard put up and took away several more Cézanne paintings. When he ran out of Cézannes, he placed other canvases in the window, cocking his head to see the reaction of his rain-soaked, one-man audience. Diego, though chilled, made no move to enter the gallery or to wipe the rain from his face. He had rooted himself to the pavement, and only the failing daylight caused him to leave.

That night, his soaked clothes flung over a chair, he came down with a high fever. His teeth chattering, he lay on his cot, not even able to eat crackers from his traveling bag without vomiting on the floor. Delirium, like the one he'd experienced from diphtheria, swept over him with its eerie sounds and sights. On the ceiling, he suddenly saw a parade of Cézanne paintings. Each canvas was more exquisite than the next in its symphony of color, its geometric blending of distance with foreground. Stumbling between the paintings were naked peasants—Mexican, Spanish, English—some with hands tied behind them, others with bullet wounds in their chests.

Diego felt that priceless secrets were being revealed to him on the ceiling—about what and how he should paint, where he should be. Through the whole night on his Paris cot, his delirium kept him from naming the secrets, making the ceiling paintings fade and the suffering peasants disappear. But something had changed for Diego. He knew now with a rush of certainty that if he kept painting like a *tonto loco*, the secrets would someday be his.

CHAPTER FIVE

◫

TWO GALLERIES HAD ACCEPTED
samples of his work! Unknown in Paris art circles,
he impressed the sedate Autumn Salon and the
newer Independents. At the Independents, Diego's painting
The House on the Bridge was wedged in among six thousand
canvases by two thousand artists, but it received good reviews. He'd spent three months grappling with painting light
on water for *The House on the Bridge*. Mailing the reviews to
his parents, he called the crowded exhibition a "sardine can"
but said he'd finally launched his "own bark."

Señor Rivera sent congratulations, enclosing an invitation
from Governor Dehesa. Would Diego come to Mexico City
for the celebration of one hundred years of Mexican indepen-
dence from Spain? All travel expenses would be paid. Diego
would surely sell paintings; the governor had displayed his

THE HOUSE ON THE BRIDGE. 1909. *This canvas brought Diego his first acceptance in a Paris art gallery, the Independents. He received fine reviews for his skill at painting light on water.* INBA—Museo Nacional de Arte, Mexico City, Mexico.

work, and President Díaz knew his name. The president, said Governor Dehesa, would lead a celebration parade in honor of Padre Hidalgo, the nineteenth-century priest who'd fought so bravely for Mexico's freedom.

Diego strolled across Paris with two friends he'd made in the academies, the artists Amedeo Modigliani and Juan Gris. They'd reveled with him in the works of Cézanne and of the ailing Frenchman Henri Rousseau, and had promised to introduce him to Picasso. "I'm going to Mexico to exhibit," he told them. "I'll return with a new hat—a Mexican sombrero."

He left by boat for Spain to pack up paintings and to see Chicharro. In September 1910, he sailed for Mexico. The torrents of flowers and wild fruit of his native land were a homecoming of color. He'd grown used to the pastels of Europe; in Mexico, along fields and dirt roads, were forest greens, stark purples, sun-hot yellows and dazzling reds. The warm brown skin of his people matched his own color.

In his parents' house on Carcuz María, Diego was embraced with happy tears. Aunt Cesaría actually managed a nod. Looking for his aunt Vicenta, he saw his mother and sister grip hands. "Aunt Vicenta died, Diego," said his father. "She left you her pottery and lacquered buckles from the old chest in her room."

"I don't go to church," Diego answered sadly, "but I will go tonight for her and light a candle."

On November 20, at Mexico's centennial celebration, President Díaz's wife purchased six of Diego's paintings—her favorite being *Pedro's Place*, a fishing scene from the Basque region of Spain. Faculty members from San Carlos bought several canvases for the workroom where Diego had studied with Rebull. Soon, all forty of his paintings were sold. Beneath the exuberance of the parade for Padre Hidalgo, however, was a familiar rumble of dissent. Peasants and students stared, stony-eyed, at Porfirio Díaz. They were less willing to wait for an end to Mexico's poverty and disease. In larger and larger numbers, they were demanding reform.

While Diego sold his paintings, Francisco Madero, a native politician who'd gathered peasant support, was using the celebration to call for an overthrow of the Díaz regime. Scarcely had festivities ended when an insurrection began, peasants setting fires on the *latifundios* (estates of the rich). Leading the peasants were the latest heroes of José Posada's *calaveras*: Pancho Villa, Pascual Orozco, and Emiliano Zapata. Hooting and hollering, risking death with a laugh, these men rode on horseback out of the forests, stirring the people against Porfirio Díaz.

By the third evening of the insurrection, Diego announced at his parents' dinner table that he would climb into the hills to join Emiliano Zapata. "If blood is to be shed in the name of justice," he said, "I'll offer to shed my own. My return to Paris can wait."

A silence fell over the table. As in the days of her son's childhood, Diego's mother made the sign of the cross. Aunt Cesaría, hastily dropping a spoon, leaped to her feet. "You and your frog eyes, Diego!" she shrieked. "Why do you always bring grief to your family? *Dios mío*, can't you ever behave? Must you die with the ignorant peasants?"

"Enough!" said Diego's father. He spoke in the same tone he'd used when, faced with Aunt Cesaría's anger, he'd promised the room of blackboards to his three-year-old son. "Diego's concerns for the poor are my own. Yet he's bolder than his father." Rising, then, from his chair, Señor Rivera leaned toward his wife's sister. "You are you, Cesaría—aging, unmarried, and childless—and, as I have told you many times, Diego is *Diego*."

Diego pulled himself up the canyon with the help of thick vines, his shoes torn by rocks. Above him, Zapata plotted strategy by a campfire. Diego felt at ease with the dark heat and the bugs; he seemed to himself like a figure in a story. Tales would be told of this chapter in Mexico's history. Some would be true, some would be false.

For five months, Diego had ridden with Zapata's peasants across the state of Morelos. They'd raided army posts for arms and ammunition and, by night, had dug up main roads traveled by soldiers. Diego had learned to camouflage himself and to shoot a gun. In other hill camps, Pascual Orozco and Pancho Villa welcomed thousands of student protesters; Francisco Madero, who'd triggered the revolt, was said to be sure enough of victory to expect the presidency.

At the top of the canyon wall, Diego shook off clumps of

mud. Zapata, he knew, would be glad to see him. He had brought a small bomb designed by an old classmate from San Carlos, hiding it beneath tubes of color in his paint box. The bomb could be exploded in a train's baggage car, sparing passengers and saving the locomotive for the rebels. Diego had hiked for miles to bring the bomb to Zapata. Though his stomach churned from eating wild berries, he felt healthier than he had in Europe.

Reaching the campfire, he exchanged greetings with the circle of disheveled but grinning men. He opened his paint box, removed the bomb, and handed it to Zapata. A glow from the fire haloed itself around Zapata's head. "More bombs can be made," Diego said.

"*Gracias*," Zapata answered, passing the bomb among his men. "You're loyal, Rivera," he said quickly. "You use a gun now almost as well as you use a paintbrush. But you can no longer stay here. Word has come that Díaz knows you've joined us. He'll issue an order for your arrest and execution for treason. I won't be responsible for your death."

Startled, Diego sat down by the fire. He'd realized he would be camping and fighting alongside the peasants for only a short time. "You must contact Antonio Rivas Mercado," Zapata said. "He works for Díaz but he respects you. The Chief of Police is his relative. Together, they will stall an arrest order until you're out of sight."

Hiking back to Mexico City, Diego met Antonio Mercado and was immediately hustled into a private carriage. Told to lie flat on the carriage floor, he heard the instructions given to the coachman: Transport this "hidden cargo" down the road to Puebla, then to Tlazcala, then to an overnight halt in the town of Apizaco. Diego was weary and dirty from his months in the hills. He slept that night on the carriage floorboards with his gun in his hand. At dawn came a train ticket to Jalapa where, hours later, Governor Dehesa greeted him at the station. "Nothing must happen to you," the governor intoned. "You'll stay with me until we book your passage for France. Your destiny, Diego, is in art, not in politics."

"The fight needs to be won here," Diego replied.

"Díaz is trapped like an old dog," the governor said. "Finished. Mexico's fight, however, will continue. Whoever comes to power may be tarnished by money or greed."

Diego let himself be led toward another carriage, heavy whorls of train smoke giving him some protection from discovery. When would the order be given for his arrest? Would a firing squad wait in every Mexican town? What the governor said, Diego thought, unfortunately made sense. If Francisco Madero were president, reforms would come—but probably not enough to solve the plight of the peasants.

He imagined himself in Paris, joking with Modigliani as they set up easels in Montparnasse or counted the coins in their pockets to see if they could eat. He must write his parents of his departure. And he would, indeed, return to France wearing a sombrero, not a cowboy hat. Perhaps, at some café table among friends, he might even be able to explain his concern for the oppressed everywhere. "Hurry, Diego!" the governor said, opening the carriage door. "The stationmaster is staring at you. We must be on our way."

Diego bent forward to climb headfirst into the carriage. Before disappearing into its cool shadows, however, he turned back toward the stationmaster, who was frowning at him under a blue-visored cap. "Do I *really* look like Emiliano Zapata, hero of the people?" Diego shouted, hoping to confuse the stationmaster and raising his hands in a defiant wave.

CHAPTER SIX

◳

HE JUMPED FROM PEASANT REV-
olution in Mexico to a revolution in art. While the
world wrestled with political and ethical "isms"—
capitalism versus communism, spiritualism versus material-
ism; while everyday life in towns and cities was being
bombarded with modern inventions—the telephone, the light
bulb, the X ray, the airplane—a new art "ism," cubism, en-
snared Paris, topping impressionism, pointillism, fauvism,
and futurism. Reducing all forms, even the human figure, to
geometric shapes, cubists painted in squares, circles, rectan-
gles, and triangles. Multiple views of one object might be
combined on the same canvas. Artists, contending with the
clash between old ways and new, sought to transform art itself. In 1906, Picasso had used cubist technique. Georges

Braque, a well-known French artist, also hailed this blending of science with art.

"Life is crazy," Modigliani told Diego on his friend's return to Paris. "Rumors of war fill Europe. Machines wipe out handiwork and artists lose favor. Yesterday, we were craftsmen and creators. Today, we're playthings of the rich, scrambling to be noticed. Cubism is our tantrum."

"But I must try it," Diego answered. "I must try everything in painting."

Diego was about to try sharing living quarters with a woman. He'd met Angelina Beloff, a Russian artist, before leaving Paris, drawn to her blue eyes and the gentle, birdlike tilt of her head. She was older than he by six years, calm and maternal toward him. "You're true to your name, Angelina," he'd said. "You're an angel. I'm a heathen."

Angelina kept order among canvases, dirty clothes, and paint tubes while Diego produced more than one hundred paintings. He kept experimenting with various techniques, using sand and wax for texture or concentrating on emerald greens. He searched for the secrets he'd almost named in his fever in the Hotel Suez. If discovery still eluded him, he tried not to torment Angelina. Instead, he'd fling open a window and yell down in Spanish at passersby. In a fit of what he called "black spirits," he cut up his sombrero into dozens of "cubist pieces."

Paris galleries continued to show his work. Wealthy patrons commissioned him to do portraits, surprised by his informality. No one had to sit stiffly in a chair for him; his subjects could move about the room, smoke, take a walk. Diego painted amazing likenesses of them. Ramón Gómez de la Serna, a writer, returned from a stroll to find his portrait "looking much more like me than when I went out. . . ."

Art critics, however, did not always respond kindly to Diego. Some treated him with silence or called him the Mexican Cowboy, not "refined" enough for the Paris art world. In 1914, when the Weill Gallery gave him his first one-man show, Parisian reviewers stayed away. That same year, having dived into cubism, he heard that one of his cubist works in a Madrid shop had stunned passersby into blocking traffic. Cubism was strange to the Spanish public; aside from some scornful laughter, they, too, remained silent.

Diego ignored the whims of public taste, but he was more dependent now on selling paintings. Francisco Madero, who had finally succeeded Díaz as Mexico's president, had been murdered. A military general, Victoriano Huerta, seized the presidency, appointing new officials. Diego lost the yearly stipend that paid his rent. Like so many artists, he teetered on the edge of poverty. His friends brought him food and supplies whenever they sold paintings. If he had money, he and Angelina invited other artists to meals until money ran out— or until Modigliani, who was drinking heavily, caused a fight that sent everyone home.

In 1914, World War I struck Europe, pitting the Allies— which included Great Britain, France, Italy, Japan, and Russia—against the Central Powers—which included Germany and Austria-Hungary—and causing a shortage of food and fuel. During enforced nightly blackouts in Paris, Diego could light neither candle nor lamp. For three war-torn years, he painted until evening shadows swallowed the last patch of daylight, then paced his room until Angelina recited poems to calm him. One night, he couldn't bear to leave his canvas. Squinting in the darkness, he added white paint to a cubist rendering of the Eiffel Tower. How, he wondered, could he stop painting? Tilting his palette toward the window, he reached out for a last shard of light.

The paint seemed to disappear in the darkness. Diego dipped a finger across what he knew was white pigment. Sighing, he thrust his finger in his mouth, letting paint smear over his tongue. Better to paint *something*, he thought. If the war did not end, the blackouts would rob him of countless hours of painting time. "Diego," said a soft voice at his side. "Come sit. Or sleep. You'll paint tomorrow."

"Tomorrow, Angelina, is always too late."

Laying her palm across his forehead, Angelina nodded. In a hesitant, lilting whisper, she began to sing an old nursery rhyme. Tired, Diego put down his palette. "When I was small and sick," he said in surprise, "my aunt Vicenta sang that rhyme. But it has no place in wartime Paris—or in an artist's sorrows."

"Oh, but it does, Diego," Angelina said.

Puzzled, he turned toward the slender frame of this woman who shared his bed. For a moment, he imagined painting Angelina on a crate by the door, contrasting her softness with rough wood. "What are you saying?" he finally asked.

"I'm pregnant, Diego," she told him. "I'm going to have your child."

Reeling, he fought against a scream. *No!* The war was enough. His search for answers was enough. He had no space for a child, no money to feed it. It would cry day and night, steal Angelina, disrupt his painting. No! He must not allow it. He would hurl it from the window. But, Diego thought in alarm, it was already here, wasn't it?—hiding in its maternal cave, waiting to destroy him.

World War I expanded, pulling in the United States on the side of the Allies. It was 1917, a year that would pull at Diego as well. Russia, land of Angelina's birth, thundered with two revolutions against czarist rule. Mexico, governed by Venustiano Carranza since General Huerta's assassination, partially soothed its peasant revolutionaries, at least on paper, with a Liberal constitution. In the cafés, trying to forget the swell of Angelina's abdomen, Diego talked less to other artists than to Spanish and French anarchists and Russian refugees. Revolution and its dreams of freedom seemed safer to him than being responsible for a baby. Diego could almost smell the muddy Mexican hills where he'd camped with Zapata. His stories of gunfights and sabotage grew larger and larger at each retelling. He had been a bandit, a spy, a conspirator, he assured the anarchists; didn't they believe him?

Diego's son, whom he named Diego, was born before the

end of 1917. Pale and shivering in winter's bleakness, the baby lay under threadbare blankets. Water was frozen in the pipes and pumping stations of Paris. Diego worried about the child he hadn't wanted; in spite of its small, throaty cries and spitting, he actually loved it. Besides, the baby was too small to disturb him by rummaging in his paints. It seemed too small, also, to survive the unrelenting cold of wartime January and February.

Angelina fussed over the child, her blue eyes moist with tears. In the mornings, Diego would leave the studio for an hour, promising Angelina to ask friends for milk. Yet if he visited Modigliani, there would be only wine or beer. Picasso, now his friend, would slip him money for the "war baby." Diego's admiration for Picasso was intense. Even when they quarreled, he called him "Master."

Cubism, carried by Picasso as a torch, had begun to plague Diego. He liked only one of his own cubist canvases and had painted it without planning it. *Zapata Landscape* didn't look European; its sombrero, colored shawl, and volcanic peaks were purely Mexican, its rifle a reminder of Mexico's revolution. The title of the work paid homage to Zapata. "You're homesick, Diego," Angelina said when she saw the canvas.

Diego's homesickness grew. Although World War I was

ZAPATA LANDSCAPE—THE GUERRILLA. 1915. *Painted in Paris during Diego's cubist phase while revolution raged in Mexico. Emiliano Zapata, Diego's hero, is represented here against a landscape of the Valley of Mexico.* INBA— Museo Nacional de Arte, Mexico City, Mexico.

ending—with artillery damage being repaired in Paris—fuel and good food were still luxuries. A fall freeze weakened Diego and Angelina's son. Milk was still so scarce that the baby was undernourished. By January it developed a high fever, but although a doctor was summoned, nothing could be done; the child died in its mother's arms. Grief-stricken, Diego felt torn from any ties to either Paris or Angelina. For weeks, he dreamed fitfully of Mexico. "I must go home," he told Modigliani, knowing that his friend, sick from too much wine, would also soon die.

In one dream, Diego saw himself on the hills of *Zapata Landscape* while a beautiful woman named Mexico, roses twined in her hair and castanets on her fingers, danced for him. "Paint me, Diego!" she called, laughing. "Paint me on walls of buildings, on chapels and churches! Tell my story! Let everyone see me who walks the land."

Awake, Diego was suddenly obsessed. As if his son's tragic death had opened a door, he could envision the saga of Mexico as his own voice in paint. Walls could be filled with painted tales of ancient Aztecs and Mayans, of holy serpents and blood sacrifice. He might retell the sixteenth century's Spanish conquest of Mexico, with its brazen cruelties and stolen land. Hungry peasants and bandit heroes could be painted; scenes could unfold of murder and assassination, of

LA PIÑATA. 1953. *The holiday piñata, filled with gifts, is a favorite of Mexican children. This mural is in the Children's Hospital of Mexico.* Hospital Infantil de México, Mexico City, Mexico.

FLOWER DAY. 1925. *This canvas by Diego won the top prize at the Pan-American exhibit at the Los Angeles Museum and became extremely popular in the United States.* Los Angeles County Museum of Art, Los Angeles County Fund.

THE TOTONAC CIVILIZATION. 1950. *One of Diego's historic panels at the National Palace, depicting an ancient Indian people who lived in Mexico's Veracruz area.* Palacio Nacional, Mexico City, Mexico.

celebration and love. The story of the Mexican people—their pain, joy, and pride—might be a permanent art and architecture in the land.

Walls! Diego told himself. *I must paint walls!* Arranging a meeting with David Alfaro Siqueiros, a Mexican artist-revolutionary visiting in Paris, he reminded Siqueiros of the mural paintings in the Aztec city of Teotihuacán in the third and fourth centuries. "We can renew our mural tradition!" Diego exclaimed. "We'll choose our own themes. We'll paint peasants and laborers struggling to survive. *Politics and art can blend!*"

Siqueiros was eager to help reawaken a mural movement. "But first," Diego cautioned him, "I must go to Italy, where murals are part of classic art. I will study day and night."

"And cubism?" Siqueiros asked.

"I renounce it!" Diego said. "Yesterday I saw ripe peaches in an old pushcart. I wanted to paint them as they were—no cubist shapes—just a mound of delicious yellow fruit."

Bidding good-bye to all his friends and to Angelina—who had been mastering Spanish so she might follow him to Mexico even though he'd not invited her—Diego left for Vienna, Ravenna, Pompeii, and Rome. For seventeen months, he studied famous frescoes, wall and ceiling murals painted on layers of wet plaster by fifteenth-century artists such as Michelangelo, Raphael, and Paolo Uccello. He beheld the

THE BANDIT AUGUSTIN LORENZO. 1936. Instituto Nacional de Antropología e Historia, Mexico.

57

magnificent mosaics in the great churches, filling his sketch-books with over three hundred drawings and learning the technical aspects of mural work. The materials used for frescoes gave them the permanence of architecture.

In July 1920, Diego left Italy for Mexico. He felt no need to search further for his voice. Walls awaited him in his native land. Although his eleven years in Europe had broadened his skills in drawing and painting, carrying his work into galleries, art studios, and private homes, he had not really been a European artist. He was, he would agree with his French critics, a Mexican Cowboy—more devoted, however, to paintbrush than gun. If he missed Angelina and his dead son, if he were to grow apart from Modigliani, Picasso, and Gris, he was still going—*home.*

"Good-bye, Europe!" he bellowed upon boarding the ship to Mexico. "Good-bye, Italy; good-bye, France. Good-bye, Spain."

Within his good-byes, Diego certainly never dreamed that his monumental revival of mural painting in Mexico would ignite fires of controversy and bring him enduring fame.

CHAPTER SEVEN

◻

THE SCAFFOLD, BALANCED ON
two ladders, sagged under his weight. On his palette
he stirred iron-oxide paint. *Walls*. If he'd wanted
walls, he had them. They stretched above him, beneath him,
beyond him; three stories high, two blocks long, one block
wide. The courtyard of Mexico City's Ministry of Education
building. A vast "canvas" for his work.

Diego had been hired by José Vasconcelos, Minister of Education, to help "dignify Mexico." Ten years of revolution, of
beggars, bandits, and soldiers, of broken promises by presidents soon murdered or overthrown, had ravaged bridges and
rails and left schools, hospitals, and orphanages in disrepair.
"I'll give you walls, Rivera," Vasconcelos had said. "You'll

paint for the people who cannot read or write. You'll inspire leaders to teach them."

Mexico, in spite of poverty and distress, had looked exquisite to Diego. The minister had assigned him a wall at the National Preparatory School in Mexico City, but his joy was cut short when his father fell ill. Between bedside vigils with his family, Diego had managed to calculate the wall's dimensions. On the day his father died, he stood before the wall in silent homage. The one thousand square feet to be painted reminded him of the blackboards. "Now, Papa," he whispered, "I have a giant blackboard to fill."

Using water-resistant colored oxides of manganese, iron, aluminum, and copper, Diego had tested the fusion of each color with the lime and marble dust in his plaster. His studies in Italy had prepared him for frescoes. Three coats of plaster, free of salts, nitrates, or ammoniates that ruined color, were applied to a wall section. On the rough second coat, hand-drawn sketches were traced with a perforating wheel to keep them visible. Painting began as the top coat reached the proper humidity; work had to stop in six to twelve hours, when the plaster dried. By then, carbon dioxide from the air had waterproofed the paint. It would last as long as the wall did unless it was hammered, gouged, or chiseled off.

Diego had worked fifteen hours a day on his wall, forgetting to eat or eating too much. He labored a year, whitewashing sections he didn't like and plastering again. The twelve-foot-high figures on the mural represented various

Mexican races and symbolized Primal Energy, the Tree of Life, Tradition, and Knowledge. The composition often mirrored the school's structure: a curve of doorway arch was reflected in mural curves of painted halos. And Diego had been bold with color. Deep greens, brick reds, violets, and startling yellows poured from the mural's center, where a semicircle of blue sky held an array of gold stars.

Never had Mexico been so stirred by a work of art. People loved or hated Diego's wall; they were moved by its beauty or offended by its nude figures. Newspapers, journals, and church sermons praised or criticized the mural, which Diego had named *Creation*. Other artists flocked to Mexico from the United States and even from Paris, begging Minister Vasconcelos for walls. Siqueiros was hired, as was another Mexican revolutionary artist, José Clemente Orozco. It was Diego, however, whom Vasconcelos chose in 1923 for the Ministry of Education courtyard, a project so mammoth it riveted world attention on Mexican art.

Here were huge surfaces where Diego could paint what no artist had ever painted—the panoramic view of a civilization. People would be able to "read" Diego's walls without being literate; they could just walk and look at the three-story-high, two-block-long courtyard. Naming the divided wall areas *Court of Labor* and *Court of the Fiestas*, Diego had planned his murals. On the ground floor of *Court of Labor* would be Mexican workers: weavers, miners, farmers, fruit gatherers, dyers, potters, metal workers, factory hands. On the second

and third floors, he would show the growth of Mexican art: dance, drama, painting, music, poetry, sculpture.

In *Court of the Fiestas*, the walls would be used for Mexican festivals and fairs, and for folk ballads and martyrs of the revolution. Diego would paint the corn and flower festivals, the burning of mock Judases on the Saturday of Glory, the holidays of the First of May and the Day of the Dead. He would show Yaqui Indians performing dances and Mexican peasants in pagan ceremonies; he would illustrate verses from a ballad about Zapata. His colors would be heavier and darker at the building's base than on wall sections nearer the sky.

Diego contrasted Mexico's joy with its poverty. Downtrodden peasants were shown with backs bent in toil. Guerilla fighters were painted rescuing enslaved peasants while a cruel landowner, smug with money and power, stood with thumbs tucked in his cartridge-lined belt. Yet Diego wanted his murals to offer hope. Several panels would deal with the redistribution of land. Peasants, engrossed in their work, would seem lively and cheerful.

On the evening Diego sat on his sagging scaffold, stirring iron-oxide paint, he was finishing a panel for *Court of Labor*. Miners, shown lowering themselves into a mine, bore a wooden beam similar to the cross borne by Jesus. On the next panel, the miners reappeared: an exhausted face framed in the pit, a man on the ground being searched by an overseer. On timbers at the mine's exit, Diego had copied a rev-

FOUNDRY. 1923. Secretaría de Educación Pública, Mexico City, Mexico.

olutionary message from the Mexican poet Gutierrez Cruz:

Compañero minero,
doblegado bajo el peso de
  la tierra,
tu mano yerra
cuando saca metal para el
  dinero.
Haz puñales
con todos los metales,
y así,
verás que los metales
despues son para tí.

Comrade miner,
bowed under the weight of
  the earth,
thy hand does wrong
when it extracts metal for
  money.
Make daggers
with all the metals,
and thus,
thou wilt see that the metals
afterward are for thee.

Diego was wiping paint from his brush when a voice called up from the courtyard. "They cannot stay," said José Vasconcelos, his posture stiffening below the scaffold, bundles of newspapers piled at his feet.

"Climb up!" Diego called back to the minister. "What cannot stay?"

Vasconcelos gripped one of the wooden ladders. "You must chisel off Cruz's words, Diego. The newspapers are blasting us. They accuse you of encouraging mine workers to kill their bosses."

NIGHT OF THE RICH. 1926. *A scene from Diego's* Court of Labor *murals, on the Ministry of Education Building.* Secretaría de Educación Pública, Mexico City, Mexico.

"I encourage poor peasants," Diego replied, "to throw off their shackles. Isn't that justice?"

José Vasconcelos shook his head. "The government is angry. I cannot defend your walls if the words remain. I cannot stop your murals from being destroyed."

Diego shifted uneasily on the scaffold. Assistants had mixed paints and laid plaster for him, but he'd given almost every waking hour of eighteen months to the courtyard. He could be painting for years before the project was finished. His walls were like a new child. "Please, Diego," Vasconcelos urged. "Remove the words. Your own message will be seen for centuries to come. Look at your energy! This courtyard is more than most artists could paint in a lifetime."

Vasconcelos said no more, picking up his bundled newspapers and leaving. Watching him, Diego groaned. He despised giving in to the government. What would Zapata have said? Should Diego relinquish one small battle in order to not lose the war? Was the plight of Mexican miners clear without Cruz's words? "Rivera!" he seemed to hear Zapata saying. "Get rid of the words. Make a small sacrifice!"

Slowly, Diego picked up an iron hammer from the scaffold, raising it above his head. Just this once, he thought grimly, for the sake of my walls. But never, never again. With a single, heavy blow, then, he swept the hammer through the air, its two-pronged heel smashing down on the word *puñales* (daggers)—making paint, plaster, and verse crumble away.

☐　☐　☐

A new woman was in his life. Letters had arrived from Angelina, but he'd rarely written back. He cared for her but no longer loved her. She was still studying Spanish, hoping he'd send for her. She didn't mind that he'd admitted to a Parisian affair with an artist named Marievna and the birth of a little girl, Marika, whom he'd not seen. She admired him, she wrote, for contributing to the child's support. "You will write less and less if we let time run on," Angelina said in a letter. "In a few years, we will meet as strangers."

Perhaps Angelina sensed that Diego had already deserted her totally. Loving him for the rest of her life, she would eventually move to Mexico, knowing that he was not hers. In her place was Mexico's Guadalupe Marín, nicknamed Lupe, described later by Diego as a "strange and marvelous-looking creature, nearly six feet tall . . . black-haired, yet her hair looked more like that of a chestnut mare than a woman's . . . green eyes so transparent she seemed to be blind . . . extraordinary hands [with] the beauty of tree roots or eagle talons."

When Diego introduced outdoor murals to Mexico, many women—including Lupe—had stood among gaping crowds under his scaffold. Women flirted with this heavyset, bulging-eyed artist who, dressed in stained overalls, worked in plain view like ordinary bricklayers, pile drivers, and roofers. But Diego was not ordinary. A storybook of figures flowed from his brushes. "Oh, your hands are sensitive," a woman might coo, inviting him to descend his ladder for a home-cooked meal.

Even Lupe, who talked Diego into marriage in 1922, could not keep women at bay or Diego from dallying with them. Wild and tempestuous, Lupe yanked Diego's hair if she suspected he'd been with another woman—and often he had. Jealous of a lanky model, she tore up his sketches and destroyed a canvas. Yet Diego spent many of his nonpainting hours with male artists such as Siqueiros and an Indian artist, Xavier Guerrero. Together, the three men had defied government disapproval by forming the Revolutionary Union of Technical Workers, Painters, Sculptors, and Allied Trades. Declaring their allegiance to peasant rights, they'd joined Mexico's tiny Communist Party, comprised mainly of artists. They became editors of the party's newspaper, *El Machete*.

At night, while Lupe slept, Diego wrote down his "scaffold thoughts." Notebooks were crammed with his musings on politics. He wrote scattered pages on ancient Aztec art, on children's and folk art, on *pulquería* (tavern wall painting). Of Mexico's love of color, he said, "I have looked into so many houses of adobe, so old and miserable that they seemed rather to be mole holes than human habitations, and in the depths of these holes I have always seen a few flowers, a few engravings and paintings, a few ornaments . . . a religion of color."

As the Ministry of Education courtyard filled with Diego's color and art, his story of Mexico brought admiring gasps

PORTRAIT OF LUPE MARIN. 1938. *Diego's wife from 1922 to 1927.* INBA—Museo de Arte Moderno, Mexico City, Mexico.

from the public. He tried Mayan and Aztec techniques on his walls, adding water to plaster to prolong its wetness and nopal cactus juice to bind it. But water thinned his colors and the juice left stains. Italian techniques proved the most reliable, and, by early 1924, Diego's courtyard was famous among international art critics. "The Mexican fresco revival," said one critic, "is the most important development in murals since the Italian Renaissance." The Mexican Cowboy had become a celebrity.

Lupe brought basket lunches and dinners to Diego's scaffold. One evening, she appeared empty-handed, her black hair uncombed, her eyes flashing with rage. "You're shameless!" she screamed. "Your head is as fat as your stomach!"

Accustomed to Lupe's moods, Diego beamed down at her. "And my eyes are fat as a frog's, no?"

"I always forgave you for being unfaithful!" Lupe cried. "But with my own sister? How could you, Diego?"

He blinked, laying down his brush. "Sometimes I do things without thinking, Lupe—even with your sister."

Lupe stomped her foot and curled her long fingers as if to claw him. "I'm leaving you, Diego! I was going to shoot off your arm so you'd never again paint! You're a monster—a *monster*!"

Her hair flying in disarray, Lupe stormed from the courtyard. Diego would later say that his heart had lurched out of place. How could she leave him? He didn't seem able to stay faithful to one woman; fidelity in marriage wasn't even important to him. Stifling himself would be like not knowing, like painting his Mexican story only in black and white. *"Monster!"* Lupe had screamed at him, as his aunt Cesaría had screamed when he'd crayoned a red sun on the wall in his parents' house. He'd not stopped himself then, couldn't stop himself now. Was he truly some kind of monster?

If Lupe was gone, Diego consoled himself, he would follow her.

CHAPTER EIGHT

□

W HY LIVE IN PASTELS IF HE could live in high color? Why hesitate if he could jump, tell a quiet tale if he could invent a drama? Diego bought Lupe a flamboyant hat with a scarlet plume; she returned to him, posed for his wall nudes, and bore him two daughters, Guadalupe and Ruth, before ending the marriage in 1927.

As stormy as the union was, Lupe would remember Diego with love, as did Angelina. Yet across Mexico, where women were judged more strictly than men, Lupe was remembered for her jealous furies. When Diego once painted for days without sleep, he fell from his scaffold. Three assistants carried him home with a cracked skull, but Lupe thought he'd been out with a woman. "Throw him on the couch," she ordered the men. "I'll take a look when I've finished eating."

Working feverishly on the courtyard after his fall, Diego was hired to paint the auditorium at the agricultural school in Chapingo. His subject was land, its distribution to peasants, its control by good and bad government, its development by the sciences. Not all Mexicans, however, were happy with the mural movement. Under yet another president, Plutarcho Calles, a campaign of violence erupted against wall frescoes. "Rivera wants the poor to see his murals and seize power," government officials muttered. "We'll be the losers."

Frescoes painted by Orozco at Mexico's Preparatory School were gouged with jackknives and defaced by scratched-in obscenities. Vandals used hatchets on murals by Mexican artists Fermin Revueltes, Emilio Amero, and Fernando Leal. Although Diego's work was unharmed, local newspapers censured his heavy, dark-skinned nudes—so different from the thin, light-skinned ladies of European fashion who never toiled in the fields. Mexicans were often ashamed of their brown skins and strong bodies. They'd been taught that art concerned itself with elegance. Could a simple peasant be worthy of an artist's brush?

Praise of Diego's work in foreign journals temporarily halted the destruction of frescoes. Art experts shook their heads in amazement as they watched Diego at work. This "artist of the people," this paint-splattered Mexican Cowboy, was a curiosity. Growing fatter each year, he'd responded to vandals by carrying a pistol. He talked of communism, his stuffed sinuses, ancient Aztec idols, and world revolution all in one breath. But his art! "One sees the importance of these paintings," wrote critic Louis Gillet about the Ministry of Education courtyard, "in which Diego Rivera has created the first revolutionary imagery. . . . This is a work of which one will seek in vain for an equivalent, not only in the rest of America, but also in Europe, and in Russia. . . . An irresistible seduction sweeps criticism off its feet . . . an admirable rainbow of colors, a play of all violets, oranges, tender green, rose of fire, unfolds its scarf of delights, all the voluptuous gamut of the light of Mexico. . . ."

Grudgingly, government officials began admitting the fame of *nuestro muy discutido Diego* (our much-discussed Diego). But Diego either grinned in welcome at government officials and critics or, entrenched on his scaffold, kept his backside to them. If he wasn't in the mood for visitors, he could count on being warned of their approach by his "scout," a young, wiry girl who loitered in the courtyard, eyebrows meeting like blackbird wings above her nose. "Psssst!" the girl would call at him. "Tourists are coming!" And seeing a pretty woman beneath his ladders, she'd hiss, "Watch out! You'll be in trouble!"

"Oh, *that* girl," a painting assistant informed Diego. "That's Frida Kahlo. She's expelled from school every month! She set off a homemade bomb outside a professor's window and rode a horse down the school corridors. The headmaster lets her attend classes only because she's smart."

"A tiny devil," Diego had commented. "Someday I'll paint her."

In the midst of his massive wall projects, Diego had not forsaken canvas. Paid only a pittance for his murals by the Mexican government—about the same as two U.S. dollars a day—he sold paintings to U.S. patrons. His *Flower Day* won the top prize at the Pan-American exhibit at the Los Angeles Museum. Drawings he'd made were hung in the Galerie Beaux of San Francisco. Though he painted commissioned portraits, many of his canvases depicted Mexican peasants in open-air markets. Whatever money he earned, however, was quickly spent. If bills were paid, he sent a check for his child in Paris or helped out hard-luck cases passing his way. Only rarely did he treat himself to anything, usually a piece of Aztec sculpture. He'd pay for a favored object with the last cash in his pockets, a habit that infuriated Lupe before she left.

The Communist Party had been impressed when Diego joined them; he was outspoken, talented, and increasingly famous. His editorial skills had strengthened the Party newspaper. Difficult as it was to know whether he was spouting fables or reciting facts, he spun words with such fervor that converts rushed to join the party. Still, party officials grumbled that he did not follow rules. Required to attend three meetings each month, he was repeatedly absent. Scheduled to make a speech, he might appear—or he might not. "Diego," a member climbed up Diego's scaffold to scold him, "you were to speak tonight on pressuring President Calles for land reform."

"Oh?" Diego answered, shifting reluctantly from his walls. "I'm painting. I forgot."

By 1924, Diego attended meetings so infrequently that he was asked to resign from the party. Shocked at first, he knew that art would always claim his deeper loyalty. In contrast, his friend and cohort Siqueiros had abandoned painting for politics. On an April night, Diego walked from the Communist Party meeting at which his membership had been revoked. Party officials had urged him to keep supporting them. Suddenly, from behind a clump of bushes, a dark-haired figure bolted at him. "So they expelled you!" a voice rasped. "They wanted you to do things their way, didn't they? I hope you told them they're *nothing* without Diego Rivera!"

Diego looked down at the winglike eyebrows, the petulant mouth. Frida Kahlo was now seventeen years old, nearly a woman. He glanced back toward an open window at the Communist meeting hall. "Why do you follow me, Frida?" he asked.

Defiantly lifting her chin, Frida showed a fury more brazen than Lupe's. *"Follow?"* she repeated, the word spitting out. "I do not follow—I *lead!*"

Smiling, Diego nodded. The girl was a streak of fire, a slap of heat. He would add her to one of his murals. She would not, however, be dancing with castanets; she would be dressed in the khaki shirt of a young revolutionary. He would paint her as part of Mexico's battles for social justice, part of the freedom song of peasant heroes Padre Hidalgo, Pancho Villa, Emiliano Zapata—and part of the ideals Diego himself had sought in the Communist Party, beyond its rigid, stuffy, pastel-colored rules.

Diego's writings, still scrawled at night into his notebooks, were a ground under his paintings. He wrote about revolution in Mexico and Russia. He wrote of his admiration for the technology of the United States but not for its economics; capitalism, he said, didn't give enough respect to the working masses. Some of what filled his notebooks appeared on his murals. A panel at the Ministry of Education, "Night of the Rich," caricatured U.S. capitalists J. P. Morgan, John D. Rockefeller, and Henry Ford. The painted words read:

Dan la una,	*The clock strikes one*
dan las dos,	*and then two.*
y el rico siempre	*And the rich still at it,*
pensando	*wondering*
como le hará a su	*what they can do to their*
dinero	*money*
para que se vaya doblando.	*To keep it always doubling.*

In 1927, Diego traveled to the U.S.S.R. as a guest of its government. Unreliable as he'd been about attending Communist Party meetings, the political credentials he took to

Moscow were impressive. He was now a delegate of the Mexican Peasant League, the president of Mexico's Workers' and Farmers' Bloc, and a member of the Anti-Imperialist League of the Americas. Called the "famous painter-Communist of Mexico" in the Soviet press, he was asked to paint frescoes on Moscow's Red Army building. Yet despite the hundreds of sketches he made, he never completed a fresco. Instead, he learned that many of his old Russian friends from his Paris days had been exiled from the Soviet Union for being cubists, futurists, or impressionists. Lecturing at the Russian Academy of Fine Arts, Diego frankly stated his criticisms of Soviet art. Before long, he was "requested" to return to Mexico—as he'd once been "requested" not to return to school.

With his murals at Chapingo completed, Diego put the last touches to the courtyard at the Ministry of Education. Driving himself as usual to paint long into the night, he had bouts of sinus trouble and weakness in his legs. In Moscow, saddened by Lupe's divorce proceedings, he had been hospitalized for a cough. Then, at the courtyard in Mexico, Frida turned up with bottled remedies and a string-tied package. "I have something to show you," she said.

"Why are you limping?" Diego asked her.

"None of your business."

"Frida!" he boomed. *Why are you limping?*

It was, she finally admitted, the result of a bus accident. A rod had pierced her pelvis; her foot and leg were damaged. "While you were away," she said, "the doctors expected me to die. I fooled them. Next they put me in a cast, strapped me to a board, and predicted I'd never walk again. It took me all the months you were gone—but I'm here."

"That's terrible," Diego said, bending to look more closely at her.

"Forget it!" she replied testily. "I was bored in the hospital. I ordered an easel, paints, and canvases. I've had no training, but I want your opinion of what I've done. I want the truth."

The small canvases Frida unwrapped were painted in a fine and delicate style. Diego spent several moments in silence, holding each canvas, studying carefully. "You are extremely good," he said at last. "I'll help. You must paint more."

Soon, Diego was appearing on Sundays at Frida's home in nearby Coyoacán. He might find her perched dangerously high in an orange tree or making faces at him from the patio. Her father, suspecting that Diego Rivera was somehow smitten with his daughter, warned him that Frida was a *demonico oculto* (hidden devil). Diego only laughed. As planned, he had painted Frida in khaki on a panel at the courtyard. Talking to her, he found her opinions of his work refreshing. He'd been sought out again by the Communist Party and suggested Frida join the Young Communist League. She behaved with restraint when she was introduced to Lupe and to little Guadalupe and Ruth. Later, after Lupe had made a disastrous second marriage and spoke longingly of Diego, Frida tweaked Diego's nose, called him her favorite *carasapo*—Aunt Cesaría's "frog face"—and told him his "beautiful ugliness" would always attract women.

Frida would be the touchstone in Diego's life. They married

in 1929, when Frida was nineteen. Through later divorce, re-marriage, Diego's continued infidelity to which a hurt Frida responded in kind, and agonizing surgeries on Frida's spine and leg, they would keep their bond. In the mid-1920's, and in spite of the anticapitalism in his murals, Diego's fame had intensified in the United States. A sketch he'd made in the U.S.S.R. was used for a cover of *Fortune* magazine; some of his drawings appeared in *Cosmopolitan*. American artists studied under him, returning to U.S. cities to demand walls on which to paint. Private collectors snatched up his mural sketches while the press gossiped over his life or critiqued his "revolutionary art." In the year Diego first married Frida, the American Institute of Architects, deeply impressed with his frescoes, awarded him the Fine Arts Gold Medal; for only the second time in its history they'd chosen a foreigner.

Throughout Mexico, Diego's murals were a gathering place for the illiterate poor. Mingling among collectors, artists, teachers, merchants, clerics, and critics who came to view Diego's work were hordes of the peasants he'd championed. They saw his compassion, even his defiance on their behalf, emblazoned across his murals; they felt his hope and respect. He, in turn, wanted them to know that art was not just a province of the rich but could speak to and for them, could change their lives.

FRIDA AND DIEGO RIVERA. 1931. *An oil painting by Frida Kahlo, Diego's wife from 1929 to 1939 and 1940 to 1954.* San Francisco Museum of Modern Art, Albert M. Bender Collection, Gift of Albert M. Bender.

A moment Diego would cherish came in the summer of 1928, when Mexican peasants, organized under the Agrarian Party, the Communist Party, and other left-wing groups, marched through Mexico City. Eighteen years had passed since revolution had begun in Mexico; during a dizzying round of presidents—Díaz, Madero, Huerta, Carranza, Obregón, Calles—peasants had fought for food, land, higher wages, education, medicine, and sanitation. On that summer day in 1928, at age forty-one, Diego stood on a corner of Avenida Madero, tracking the marching figures. Suddenly, one of the peasants saw him and shouted in triumphant greeting. "Diego Rivera!" the man roared, right arm sweeping out as if to include all the long, painful struggles for equality. "Here, Diego—right here on these streets, in this city, in this march—*are your paintings!*"

Diego lifted his head. His huge eyes misted over. Perhaps, he thought, in this moment of upheaval on Avenida Madero, art and life had truly become one.

CHAPTER NINE

◫

DAYS OF SUN WERE FOLLOWED BY
storms. First came the surprise: Diego was elected
Director of the San Carlos Academy of Fine Arts, the
school from which he'd once been expelled. Although his
whirlwind reforms for broadening the curriculum so threatened old-style professors that he lost the post after eight
months, his impact caused the next director to applaud "the
revolutionary program of Diego Rivera."

Government officials, trying now to win Diego's favor, offered him a cabinet post—which he refused. He was deluged
with foreign and domestic letters asking for advice, training,
or money, telling of donations to schools and orphanages in
his name, sometimes denouncing his communist beliefs or
his sympathy toward the "Mexican monkeys," the peasants.

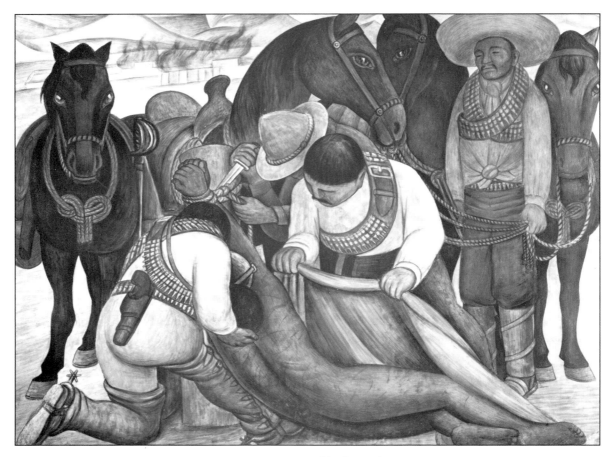

LIBERATION OF THE PEON. 1931. *A movable fresco by Diego, based on a panel of the same title in the* Court of Labor *murals on the Ministry of Education Building, and showing his concern for the plight of the peasants.* Philadelphia Museum of Art: Given by Mr. and Mrs. Herbert Cameron Morris.

New commissions were frequent. He was to design scenes and costumes for *H.P.*, a ballet opening in Philadelphia under Leopold Stokowski, the world-famous conductor. He would create frescoes for Mexico's Ministry of Health building and, at the request of the U.S. Ambassador to Mexico, Dwight W. Morrow, for the Palace of Cortés in Cuernavaca.

Diego was also awarded walls at the National Palace in Mexico City. He considered this project, when completed, his finest work. He broke new ground here as he painted the breadth of Mexican history. In Europe, murals had contained isolated scenes and figures, but Diego's palace figures, numbering in the thousands, were connected by their roles in history. "Nothing was solitary," he'd say of this political poem to his people. He further researched the Spanish conquest of Mexico in order to make no errors. He would add to these murals in 1955—twenty-six years after he began them!

In 1930, Diego received an invitation to travel to the United States to do a mural for San Francisco's Stock Exchange. Frida, married to him for one year, was ecstatic. "An adventure, *carasapo*!" she exclaimed. "You are so famous, your jabs at America don't ruin you! Let's go!"

On shipboard, Frida painted a portrait of herself as a gift to Diego. In San Francisco, the couple was treated like Hollywood celebrities. Diego's tall fleshiness towered over Frida, but she managed to grab attention with her Mexican clothing. When Diego wasn't at the Exchange, painting the huge figure of a woman to represent California, he escorted Frida on a constant round of parties, receptions, and lectures. He was sometimes morose in the face of her excitement. He wanted to paint, not to party.

In 1931, New York's Museum of Modern Art presented one hundred fifty pieces of Diego's work in a one-man show. Only Henri Matisse, the famous French artist, had enjoyed the same honor at the two-year-old museum. Although America was still reeling from the Great Depression that had begun in 1929, Diego's exhibit was popular. Returning to Mexico, he performed the amazing feat of painting a sixty-five-foot-high, forty-five-foot-wide panel at the National Palace in only three and a half months.

Still another invitation arrived: Diego was asked to travel to Detroit, Michigan, auto capital of the world, to paint the "Story of Detroit Industry" at the Institute of Arts. Edsel Ford, scion of the Ford car family and head of Detroit's Arts Commission, promised $25,000 for the project. "Pack up your costumes," Diego told Frida. "We're going again."

In Detroit, they stayed at the Brevoort Hotel. Diego, who still loved machines as he had in Guanajuato, was eager to paint what he called "the wonderful symphony of factories." Machines, he said, provided "liberation from drudgery and poverty." Machines were products of human intelligence, harnessing or overcoming the forces of nature. If a bowl of fruit, a landscape, or a nude body were "food for the artist," why not a machine? Diego spent months studying Detroit's industry, making thousands of sketches of "towering blast furnaces, serpentine conveyor belts, impressive scientific laboratories, busy assembly rooms." He walked for miles through the factories of Ford, Chrysler, Edison, and Parke-Davis. He would paint the walls of the Institute's mezzanine room into an intricate tapestry of machine pipes, pumps, and motors, of brilliant scientific and industrial achievement.

He worked fifteen hours a day, seven days a week. The only unexpected time he took off was when Frida, bleeding and rushed to a hospital, suffered a miscarriage. Injuries from the bus accident had proved too severe for tolerating extra weight in her pelvis. Devastated, Frida turned again to her own painting, retelling on canvas the pain of loss.

As Diego's murals covered the mezzanine walls at the Institute, he could feel shock waves among early viewers who tiptoed between ropes, scaffolds, and ladders. Wealthy, well-dressed women, acting as if they'd been assaulted by industry's smoke and noise, peered in horror at the vast rendering of machines. An upper panel showed hands breaking up through earth with minerals and metals. Two nudes reclined above the hands, one black-skinned to represent coal, one red-skinned to represent iron. Seeing the nudity, some female patrons hid their faces in handkerchiefs.

Another panel, an ode to medical science, depicted three workers at a biochemical plant. In the foreground, a white-coated doctor and nurse were to vaccinate a baby, while a horse, cow, and sheep—animals from whose tissues many vaccines were prepared—waited nearby. The panel became ammunition for Diego's detractors: Weren't nurse, doctor, and baby, with animals of the manger, an evil portrayal of the Holy Family? Wasn't Diego Rivera dangerous? Reading criticism in the newspapers, Frida was distracted from her miscarriage by her protectiveness toward Diego. "More *tontos locos*," she growled, "live in America than in Mexico!"

South wall of Diego's Detroit industry murals, showing his admiration for the "symphony" of American machines and technology. 1933. The Detroit Institute of Arts, Founders Society Puchase, Edsel B. Ford Fund and Gift of Edsel B. Ford.

The biggest storm against Diego came from a fanatical priest, Father Charles Coughlin. On his Detroit radio show, Father Coughlin branded Diego's murals as "obscene, filthy, and communistic." The entire city was caught up in controversy. A councilman found the murals "a travesty on the spirit of Detroit," urging that they be struck from the walls.

Even while Edsel Ford and a contingent of university professors and writers supported Diego, politicians from as far away as New York condemned him. Several days before the public presentation of the murals, four society ladies stopped Diego on the street. The soot of factories, protested the women, did not represent Detroit. Why hadn't Diego painted scenes of outdoor concerts or gardens?

"You ladies," Diego answered in fluent French, defiantly choosing that language over his stumbling English, "owe your personal riches to industry. Without factories, without machines, you wouldn't have your beautiful homes or your diamonds."

Diego wondered if his trips to America had been worthwhile. Yet when two hundred men marched into the mezzanine room before opening day, their spokesman shook Diego's hand. "We're engineers from Detroit's steel and automobile plants," the man said. "We're Democrats, Republicans, capitalists, communists. We've never set foot in this place, but we came to see what the fuss is about your murals. Now we understand. You're the first artist we know to recognize the workers!"

Watching Diego's face light up, the man continued. "We heard that hoodlums might destroy your murals. We've organized a guard to protect them. Eight thousand men have volunteered! To stay legal, we sent a letter of intent to the Governor of Michigan."

On Sunday, when the public lined up at the Institute's front doors, the guard of workers asked everyone to sign their names and addresses in a register. Frida and Diego stood nearby while crowds filed past them. So many people arrived to view the exhibit that, in an unprecedented move, the Institute staff admitted them until half past one in the morning. After the doors were finally locked, a mechanic from Chrysler's automobile plant showed Diego the swollen register. "Look!" the man said, almost gasping as he pointed to a tally written at the bottom of a page. In spite of the slurs cast against Diego and the threats to destroy his industry murals, his walls in Detroit had been seen on opening day by eighty-six thousand people.

Nelson D. Rockefeller, Jr., of New York City, known for his wealth and political connections and later to become governor of New York and a U.S. vice president, was not to be outdone by Edsel Ford. Picasso, Matisse, and Diego were approached with a mural project at Rockefeller's seventy-story RCA building in Rockefeller Center. All three artists were asked to submit samples but considered themselves well-known enough to refuse to "audition." Rockefeller was determined to secure at least Diego's services and offered him $21,000. The theme for the 1,071-square-foot wall was: Man at the Crossroads Looking with Hope and High Vision to the Choosing of a New and Better Future.

In March of 1933, missing the small home they'd built in Mexico City, Diego and Frida left Detroit for New York. The mural wall faced the main entrance of the RCA Building and had been prepared by Diego's assistants: plaster coatings traced and stenciled with his sketches, paint colors readied. Checking into the Barbizon Plaza hotel, Diego immediately began work. Through March and early April, reporters from many cities and towns kept appearing beneath his scaffold to write accounts of this unfolding marvel of a story upon a wall. Soon, Diego's audiences were so big that tickets were issued to see him paint.

By mid-April, the mural was nearly finished. A globe represented the dynamics of chemistry, biology, and physics. A telescope was shown for its revelation of bodies in space, along with a microscope for its magnification of cells, germs, bacteria, and tissue. Life-giving soil gave rise to two visions of civilization. To the right, Diego had painted various evils: a nightclub filled with the lazy rich; a battlefield with tanks, planes, bayonets, and war-shattered men; a political demonstration with unemployed laborers being clubbed by police. To the left were Diego's hopes for the future: a socialist land aglow with equality, peace, love, red banners, and singing workers, and the figure of Vladimir Ilyich Lenin, chief leader of Russia's 1917 Revolution and of the first years of Soviet government, clasping hands with a black worker, a white worker, and a soldier.

Management at Rockefeller Center agonized over Lenin's likeness on the wall. Yet Nelson Rockefeller, who had seen Diego's original sketches of Lenin, sent him a note saying,

"Everybody is most enthusiastic about the work which you are doing." Storm clouds didn't really form until April 24, when a *World-Telegram* headline announced:

RIVERA PAINTS SCENES OF COMMUNIST ACTIVITY AND JOHN D. JR. FOOTS BILL.

Diego, painting now at breakneck speed as if he sensed the fury of the storm, received another note of a different nature from Nelson Rockefeller. The face of Lenin, said Rockefeller, must now be removed and replaced with the face of an unknown man. After talking with Frida, who swore at the "gangleader of the capitalists," and with his assistants, who threatened to strike if he compromised his work, Diego dug in his heels. One change, he agreed, might lead to demands for others. And hadn't he promised himself "never again" when hammering off Cruz's words at the Ministry of Education?

The face of Lenin, Diego wrote to Rockefeller, must stay. An artist should not betray his voice. He proposed *adding* a scene of Abraham Lincoln freeing the slaves, surrounded by American heroes John Brown, Nat Turner, and Harriet Beecher Stowe. Awaiting Rockefeller's third reply, Diego believed "something terrible was about to happen." On May 9,

Diego on a scaffold, sketching his Rockefeller Center mural before he was ordered by Nelson Rockefeller to stop work because of a likeness of Lenin in one of the frescoes. 1933. AP/Wide World Photo.

The screen ordered by Nelson Rockefeller, covering the offending section of Diego's mural at Rockefeller Center. 1933. AP/Wide World Photo.

as night fell over the RCA building, the storm broke like a "flame of battle."

Three crews of gun-toting men surrounded Diego's scaffold. He was issued a check and told to stop work. The men began covering the mural with thirty-foot-high frames of stretched canvas. The building's entrance was closed off with a thick curtain, mounted policemen patrolled nearby streets, and airplanes roared over the skyscraper that Rockefeller now said was "menaced by the portrait of Lenin."

Within an hour, city workers in sympathy with Diego arrived to stage a demonstration. By morning, sides had been taken in the battle. Although conservatives labeled Diego an "agent of revolution" and an "agitator and propagandist," and Harry Watrous, president of the National Academy of Design, called Lenin's likeness "unsuitable" for an American mural, hundreds of artists, writers, businessmen, and blue-collar workers wired their support. H. L. Mencken, the renowned writer, and Rockwell Kent, the celebrated artist, both urged Rockefeller to reconsider his stand.

A *New York Times* headline proclaimed Diego Rivera the "Fiery Crusader of the Paint Brush." Protesters in riot cars sped up elegant Fifth Avenue, and demonstrators picketed the RCA building, shrieking "We want Rivera! Save Rivera's art!" Hundreds of newspapers carried the story of a seven-year-old girl who had been brutally struck by a policeman's club during one demonstration. Only the Communist Party, which had twice embraced and expelled Diego, was mute.

Diego spoke out on New York radio station WEVD. What if, he asked listeners, a millionaire bought the Sistine Chapel with its masterpieces by Michelangelo? Would that millionaire have the right to destroy the chapel? What if a millionaire bought unpublished manuscripts containing mathematical theories by a scientist like Einstein. Would that millionaire have the right to burn the manuscripts? "We all recognize," Diego said, "that in human creation there is something which belongs to humanity at large, and that no individual owner has the right to destroy it."

But destroying Diego's mural is exactly what Nelson Rockefeller did. Although he pledged on May 12, 1933, that "the uncompleted fresco of Diego Rivera will not be destroyed, nor in any way mutilated . . ." the mural was smashed to powdered dust beginning at midnight on February 9, 1934. Experts had suggested how to remove the mural, plaster intact, for preservation elsewhere. *Harper's Magazine* had advised Americans not to fear looking at Lenin's picture, since his fiercest opponents couldn't deny his place in a great mural depicting "Man at the Crossroads." Nevertheless, Rockefeller's battalions had moved in for the kill. In the enormous scandal that followed, many artists withdrew their work from New York City exhibits. Irene Herner de Larrea, a Mexican professor of history and an author of art books, linked Adolph Hitler's book burnings in Berlin, Germany, with "paradise lost in Rockefeller Center."

Diego, accompanied by a fuming Frida, held a news conference in Times Square. His bulging eyes roving over the crowds of reporters, he vowed to use any money left over from Nelson Rockefeller's check to paint a similar mural in New York "free of charge except for the actual cost of materials." The Mexican Cowboy who'd been ordered by one of America's richest men to erase the likeness of a dead world leader, the revolutionary artist who'd once joined the people's forces of Emiliano Zapata, was certainly not to be vanquished.

CHAPTER TEN

▣

WHILE STILL IN NEW YORK, Diego received a note from Dr. Élie Faure, an old friend from Paris. "I envy you," Faure wrote, "your power to awaken in the heart indignation."

Disputes, indignation, and awe over Diego's work kept his name in the headlines. Stalking the city streets, he chose the New Workers' School for his "revenge mural." The ramshackle building was actually too small for re-creating the mural at Rockefeller Center, so Diego painted instead *Portrait of America*, a depiction of America's rich and poor. Later, he brought his "murdered painting" back to life at Mexico's Palace of Fine Arts, making one addition: a likeness of Nelson Rockefeller in the nightclub scene, near a slide of deadly germs.

More than art blazed across Diego's walls. Pictured along

with the lyrical color of his stories of Mexico and other lands were his politics and opinions. The Rockefeller scandal cost him a General Motors commission at the World's Fair in Chicago, but he caused a new uproar. Painting panels at Mexico's Hotel Reforma, he showed a fictional General Marrano robbing his dance partner, Señorita Mexico, of fruit from her basket. Since the general, whose name meant "Pig," looked like Mexico's current president, Lázaro Cárdenas, the worried hotel owner repainted the figure. Enraged at another sabotage, Diego stormed the hotel, carrying three pistols. He spent a night in jail for "breaking and entering" but eventually won two thousand pesos in a Mexican court for having his work "falsified."

Diego's beloved Mexico was still beset by injustice. Though Plutarcho Calles, Mexico's president from 1924 to 1928, had redistributed some land and had given Indians equal status with mixed-blood *mestizos* and *criollos*, people of Spanish descent, peasants remained poor. The government was more tolerant of labor groups, but workers' strikes were often crushed, their defiant leaders shot or sent to the penal colony of Islas Marías.

Diego continued to hearken to the needy. He emptied his pockets to hungry peasants, paid the way home for many compatriots living unhappily in the United States, and bought chickens and cows for struggling farmers. Distracted though he was by his painting, he never forgot to help provide for his Parisian daughter, Marika, or for Guadalupe and

Ruth. He kept contributing to the Communist Party. "It's my paintings—and justice—I try to save," he told Frida. "Not money."

In 1939, as World War II began, Diego was still causing indignation. The U.S.S.R. had exiled one of its radical leaders, Leon Trotsky; after no other country would harbor Trotsky, Diego persuaded the Mexican government to grant him legal asylum. He angered communists everywhere by letting Trotsky stay in Frida's old house in Coyoacán. "Any man," Diego said, "who is persecuted for political reasons in his own country is entitled to refuge in another country."

During the war, the German ship *Columbus* dropped anchor in Mexican waters, and Diego learned that it contained hidden guns and was being used by the Nazis to service submarines. He pressured members of the Mexican army, marines, and police, and British and French legations into searching the ship—and agreed to stand trial if his charges were wrong. The *Columbus* fled out to sea and was blown up by its own crew. Later, Diego received a letter of commendation from President Franklin Roosevelt, asking if he would do a radio broadcast on Nazi terrors at sea.

The war's somber mood seemed, at times, to burrow inside Diego. He'd reached his mid-fifties a creator of visual wonders. When his energies flowed, he would paint with great gaiety, spouting his tall tales, but more often his "black spirits" descended. He had lived under two world wars and participated in revolution. He'd fought other battles on behalf of his art. Half a dozen of his family members had died, including his mother, and he had premonitions of his own death. "Before the end," he told Frida, "I want two things: to paint a glorious Tenochtitlán, Mexico's ancient capital, as it was before the Spanish conquest—and to build a small museum for my collection of pre-Conquest sculpture."

Frida, as always, would raise up her winglike eyebrows. She might speak from a hospital bed, having endured other operations on her damaged pelvis and leg. Diego would sit devotedly by her side or, if he was painting, not turn up for days. They had been divorced in 1939 and remarried in 1940. Frida worried more over Diego's health—he had developed liver trouble and rheumatism—than about her own. When she was hospitalized to see if her leg should be amputated to avoid gangrene, Diego lay in an adjoining room with an eye infection. Ignoring her possible disfigurement, Frida wept over Diego. "He mustn't go blind!" she raged to friends. "The world will lose its own eyes!"

"Frida Kahlo," said Diego after he'd recovered and was painting a wall at Mexico's Medical School, "is the little child of my soul."

Diego accomplished both of his goals: given additional walls at the National Palace, he painted the Golden Age of the Aztecs, its sacred harvests and rituals, its teeming markets and temples, its capital city, Tenochtitlán, protected by the *zopilote*, a scavenging vulture who kept the ancient world clean. On a tract of land owned by Frida, he built a pyramid-shaped stone museum for his collection of sculptures, designing and helping construct it himself. Housed on three floors were thousands of pre-Conquest art objects—ancient idols, images, and carved masks that had become valuable.

Frida had given Diego title to the land under his museum. As she grew weaker from her surgeries, she depended heavily on him. Her own paintings, each one a scene from her life, had found many European and U.S. admirers, including Picasso, and in 1953 the Mexican officials awarded her a one-woman show. On opening night, Frida arrived by ambulance, presiding over the exhibit in a wheelchair. Bravely, she'd worn one of her gaudiest, most festive outfits. Later that year, doctors finally amputated her leg; her bones had decayed beyond repair.

On July 13, 1954, Frida's lungs filled with fluid and she died. Diego seemed to grow old in a few moments. Never at a loss for words, he turned away when reporters clamored after him. "I beg of you," he said at last, "don't ask me anything."

He tried to keep busy by setting up Frida's house as a memorial museum of her work, placing her ashes there in an urn. He smiled at the baby girl born to his architect-daughter Ruth and contacted two of his old cohorts: Orozco, who'd painted murals in New York, California, and New Hampshire, and Siqueiros, whose politics were so radical that he'd fled to California to teach fresco technique. A sense of the past gripped Diego. He'd reapplied to the Communist Party, only

SELF-PORTRAIT. 1940. *An oil painting by Frida Kahlo representing her feelings about pain and death.* Selma and Nesuhi Ertegun, New York.

to be rejected because of his wealthy patrons and an unflattering portrait of Josef Stalin, but in September 1954 he was readmitted. "Frida would have been happy," he said. "I've tied up loose ends."

The Mexican government decided to honor Diego by sponsoring the publication of a photographic review of his nearly fifty years of work. He was now almost a national monument. Those who disputed him could still see his worth. He had become an artist-spokesman of the people, an advocate of their causes. Nelson Rockefeller himself, in spite of the scandal at Rockefeller Center, lent his collection of Diego's sketches and watercolors to an exhibition of five hundred pieces gathered from many lands at Mexico's National Institute of Fine Arts.

In 1955, a year after Frida's death, Diego announced that he had cancer. That summer, pale and thinner, he married a long-time friend, Emma Hurtado, who had become his traveling companion and nurse. Emma had been selling Diego's canvases at her Galería Diego Rivera; she left the gallery to take him to Moscow, where he spent months in a sanatorium. Returning to Mexico, he told everyone he'd been cured by "cobalt bomb" treatment.

The pace at which he worked had gradually slowed. He made several revisions to a mural he'd painted for Mexico's Del Prado Hotel, one of them on the face of himself as a ten-year-old boy. "The child's face had become old and wrinkled," Diego half joked. "I had to restore his lost youth."

In December 1956, he celebrated his seventieth birthday. Mexico celebrated along with him, people gathering outside his San Angel studio to wish him well. Cards and letters arrived by the thousands, including greetings from Angelina and Lupe. He began a portrait of his granddaughter and catalogued the sculptures in his pyramid-museum. The next September, a blood clot developed in his right arm. Unable to paint, he said: "The brush no longer obeys me."

Without the ability to do what he loved, Diego lay in bed,

flanked by two easels of unfinished canvases. He reminisced to Emma about his childhood, remembering the purple haze on Guanajuato's hills and the loud, intriguing growl of trains. He rewove his old tales of Zapata, Picasso, and Modigliani, relived the wet afternoon in Paris when he'd stared at Cézanne's paintings, recalled the cold of the World War I winter when his son, Diego, had died. Often, Frida's name was on his lips—but Emma did not mind. "It is your painting," she told him, "that is your truest heart."

Near midnight, on November 24, 1957, Diego knew he would not leave his bed, that not even his tallest tale could fool Death. Emma hovered over him, offering to raise the bed on its motorized springs, but he murmured, "No—on the contrary, lower it." His half-finished canvases faded from him, and though he may have yearned, suddenly, to ask for his dead aunt Cesaría's blessing—even, perhaps, for her forgiveness for his sins—he slowly closed his huge eyes. Behind the lids, he could have seen swirling colors, perhaps from his walls—red of blood, brown of earth, green of leaves, blue of sky. Then the mixture of paint would have poured over him, blending with breath and pulse until the colors turned black.

"*Diego es muerto!*" was the cry across telephone wires and wire services. Doubting crowds raced through the night to Diego's studio, only to see Emma Hurtado de Rivera nod her head. "How could Diego die?" people wailed. "Diego was Mexico! Diego was forever!" But by the next day, when the body lay in a coffin in the rotunda of the Palace of Fine Arts, crowds were hushed. By Mexican custom, a death mask was taken, along with a mold of Diego's right hand. Famous politicians and artists served as guards of honor; his sister María, whom he'd often visited and telephoned, laid roses at his feet. On the following day, Emma led thousands of men, women, and children in a funeral procession, the poor and downtrodden marching among the wealthy. Farewell addresses were given and a mournful *calavera* by José Posada was sung. "The great throng," reported the newspaper *Tiempo*, "watched the [cremation] ceremony with tears in their eyes."

Diego had wanted his ashes placed next to Frida's, but government edict had them installed in Mexico City's Rotunda de los Hombres Ilustres (Rotunda of Illustrious Men). His small bank account and his personal possessions were left to Emma and to his daughters Guadalupe and Ruth. To his country went his pyramid-museum with the treasured collection of sculptures, valued later in millions of dollars, and, of course, his greatest legacy, his walls.

Outside the house in Guanajuato where Diego once crayoned the red sun, a wooden plaque hangs. "Diego Rivera," translate the printed words, "magnificent painter, born in this house, December 8, 1886." No historian will ever again study Mexico without being influenced by Diego's work. No other country has had so much of its life retold on plaster and canvas. Because of Diego, the Mexican people have come to know themselves more fully and the rest of the world is more aware of Mexico.

Diego sparked the modern renaissance of fresco painting.

By putting his murals on walls of buildings, he was able to voice and make public his deepest concerns for the rights of human beings. His art became a bold and dynamic call for equality and justice. He was an evangelist-in-paint for social reform, taking his message to the people who struggled in the fields and factories and on the streets.

As long as paint and plaster hold together, as long as walls endure, Diego Rivera will provide the world with stories, memories, and opinions in miraculous color. He appears both colossal and astonishing—and, at the same time, reachable and every day. It was Diego's father who would remind us, if he could, that Diego, after all and everything, "is . . . just *Diego.*"

AFTERWORD

◻

IN THE YEARS SINCE DIEGO'S DEATH, his mural movement has spread throughout North America from Mexico. In cities across the United States, on walls of buildings and courtyards, on viaducts, stone fences, sidewalks, and bridges, colorful murals abound. They are a "people's art"—part of their purpose is decorative, but they exist, also, as protest and provocation, as the voice of many who yearn for better education, for an opportunity to work, to find decent shelter, to put enough food on the table.

In the Hispanic section of Los Angeles, California, a tall mural speaks for the whole community. Beneath a blue likeness of the Statue of Liberty, a painted banner of Spanish words reads: *El presente es de lucha, el futuro es nuestro* (The present is a struggle, the future is ours).

Young people take an active part in painting outdoor murals. In San Francisco, Los Angeles, and New York, in Philadelphia, Detroit, and Washington, D.C., children have created murals of their hopes, dreams, joys, fears, and sorrows on brick, stone, concrete, wood, and metal. In 1989, in Chicago, five hundred schoolchildren helped paint a 520-foot mural in Grant Park. Several movable panels of this mural are housed in Chicago's Museum of Contemporary Art. Later, panels will be given to schools attended by the children who helped paint the mural.

Mexico now offers its laborers higher wages, better working conditions, and more opportunities than in its years of revolution. President Carlos Salinas de Gortari, who took office in 1988, is developing a free trade agreement with the United States, increasing the demand for Mexican products abroad and providing for more jobs and a higher standard of living for Mexicans at home. Diego Rivera always believed in and fought for his country's future; he'd envisioned the ancient splendors of the Aztecs, created in his own land, as igniting the promise of Mexico's tomorrows.

BOOKS FOR FURTHER READING

▣

Arquin, Florence. *Diego Rivera: The Shaping of an Artist, 1889–1921*. Norman, Oklahoma: University of Oklahoma Press, 1971.

De Larrea, Irene Herner, Rafael Angel Herrerias, Gabriel Larrera, and Carlos Sirvent. *Diego Rivera: Paradise Lost at Rockefeller Center*. Mexico: Edicupes, S.A. de C.V., First English Edition, 1987.

Founders' Society, Detroit Institute of Arts. *Diego Rivera*. New York: W. W. Norton, 1986.

Herrera, Hayden. *Frida*: *A Biography of Frida Kahlo*. New York: Harper & Row, 1983.

March, Gladys, with Diego Rivera. *My Art, My Life*. New York: Citadel Press, 1960.

Museum of Modern Art, Intro. by Frances Flynn Paine. *Diego Rivera*. New York: W. W. Norton, 1936.

Wolfe, Bertram D. *The Fabulous Life of Diego Rivera*. New York: Stein & Day, 1963.

MURALS IN THE UNITED STATES

San Diego Freeway (between Manchester and Century boulevards)—Los Angeles, CA

L.A. Marathon mural by Kent Twitchell. Depicts twenty-five marathon runners.

Pacific Stock Exchange—San Francisco, CA

Diego Rivera mural. Represents spirit of California.

San Francisco Art Institute—San Francisco, CA

Diego Rivera mural. Depicts construction of a modern industrial city in the United States.

State Capitol Building—Denver, CO

Alan True mural. Depicts Colorado history.

Stephenson Building—Atlanta, GA

Triumphant Celebration mural by Calvin Jones. Depicts various art forms influenced by African Americans.

Museum of Contemporary Art—Chicago, IL
Photographs of mural created in Grant Park by 500 school-children with artist Keith Haring. Chicago Public School Board owns full mural and is looking for a permanent home for it.

Highland Park High School Auditorium—Highland Park, IL
Project headed by Hector Duarte, who studied at workshop of David Alfaro Siqueiros. Created by forty Highland Park High School students.

Auditorium, Indiana University—Bloomington, IN
Thomas Hart Benton mural. Depicts scenes of social/political history of America.

Detroit Institute of Arts—Detroit, MI
Diego Rivera mural. Represents Detroit industry.

Lambert International Airport—St. Louis, MO
Black Americans in Flight mural by Spencer Taylor. First mural to recognize black aviators.

The Indian Pueblo Cultural Center—Albuquerque, NM
Mural painted by a group of internationally known Pueblo Indian artists. Depicts dancers representing various aspects of Pueblo life.

Union Square Park—New York, NY
MasterCard project in conjunction with local groups. Mural by city children depicting "their summer values."

West Salem Branch Library—West Salem, OR
Book Ends mural by Steve Ominski. Depicts books interspersed with paintings of creatures and items from nature, children observing the artist at work, and scenes from West Salem.

The Walls of Respect; The Friendly Talking Wall—Philadelphia, PA

Under the aegis of the Philadelphia Anti-Graffiti Network, this project began in 1984, using child artists instead of established adult artists. Thirty thousand young people have been involved so far.

Texas Hall of State—Dallas, TX

Murals by Eugene Savage. Depict history of Texas and regional history and culture.

Rainier National Bank Building—Seattle, WA

Mural by Richard Haas. Depicts famous historical building located near bank. Purpose was to "rescue" a historical building through the social/political impact of the mural.

The Olin Terrace Mural (on John Nolen Drive)—Madison, WI

Mural by Richard Haas. Depicts the scene in which it is set: Madison's capitol building and nearby surroundings.

INDEX

⊡

113